SONY

THEWINEBAR
2F ステーキハウス フォルクス
↓B1

レイク
コンドームなら
不二ラテックス
1515
FRIDAY

Vanishing Japan

Modern Architecture, Gone But Not Forgotten

With 169 illustrations

Naomi Pollock

T&H

Contents

Introduction

Architect Kenzo Tange in front of his Totsuka Country Club Clubhouse.

Between the 1950s and the 1990s, Japan constructed a tremendous number of large-scale buildings: city halls and civic centres; theatres and museums; gymnasiums and schools; hotels and department stores. Plus, a host of other public, cultural, academic and commercial structures. Many of these new buildings were the creations of the country's most respected architects, including Kenzo Tange, Kunio Maekawa and Junzo Sakakura as well as Kazuyo Sejima and Kengo Kuma later on. As one decade rolled into the next, the new construction reflected changing aesthetic styles and social needs but also evolving technologies and economic ups and downs. These exemplary, innovative works became statement pieces not just within their local environments but in the larger context of Japanese architecture.

Surprisingly, many of these masterworks have not stood the test of time. Many have been taken down already or are endangered, with little prospect of preservation or repurposing. Some monumental works by mid-century Modernists, such as Yoshiro Taniguchi's Hotel Okura which was finished in the run up to the 1964 Tokyo Olympics, have garnered calls for protection from the public and design professionals. But, as in the case of Taniguchi's hotel, these efforts rarely result in their survival. Not just a matter of age, more recently completed works are also vulnerable to Japan's predilection for scrap and build.

When a building comes down, however, we lose not only a physical entity. A sense of place, a link to history and a wealth of memories go with it. Every building holds a connection to the past. 'We need to recognize that architectural works, including works of functionalist design, are important not only as … works of art but also as objects that bear witness to the age,' wrote architectural historian Hiroyuki Suzuki.[1] In concrete terms, buildings are tailored to the design values, available materials and prevailing size or scale at the time of their construction. In the public eye, they become fixtures of the manmade environment; they become local landmarks that shape the unique character of neighbourhoods. On a more individual level, buildings also form the backdrops for family celebrations, employment milestones and other personally meaningful events. They become lodged in our psyches.

Another frequent casualty of building demolition is the charming pedestrian scale that characterizes many Japanese communities. High-rises may be proliferating in Tokyo, but in between, blocks of low buildings and single-family homes still comprise much of the urban fabric. Seen from above, the entire Kanto Plain, where Tokyo is located, reads as an endless sea of small, human-sized buildings.

Historically, *machiya* rowhouses, many containing the family business in front and the living quarters in back, lined many city streets. These narrow thoroughfares were social spaces where news and gossip were exchanged as well as rice and vegetables purchased. But this sort of daily life interaction is lost when the old buildings give way to road widenings or new construction. More often than not, they are replaced with something bigger or taller. Such was the case when the street in front of the home and pharmacy belonging to the family of the Pritzker Prize winner Riken Yamamoto was enlarged. 'After that, customers stopped coming, most of the shops disappeared and the historic *machiya* were replaced with small apartment buildings whose tenants worked elsewhere … the relationship between the buildings and the street disappeared', lamented the architect.[2] Though compliance with Japan's so-called Sunshine Laws preserves a modicum of sunlight at street level, the quality of human activity changes.

Kasumigaseki Building, Yamashita Sekkei Inc., 1968.

And then there is the matter of navigation. In Japan, urban address systems are modelled more like concentric circles than grids. In the middle of these increasingly smaller organizational rings are blocks of individual buildings – each one numbered in the order of completion instead of consecutively in relation to their neighbours. Unlike in the United States or Europe, street names are relatively rare and are seldom used to identify locations. Consequently, simple maps (many hand-drawn and faxed prior to the advent of smartphones) are essential for getting from point A to point B. These diagrams rely on fire stations, elementary schools, convenience stores and other visible landmarks to delineate the path. But as property is redeveloped, these nodes disappear and this organic method of moving through the city becomes challenged. It is easier than ever to get lost in a place when the familiar cues go missing.

Unsurprisingly, the reasons buildings are taken down are manifold, spanning the practical to the philosophical. Fundamentally, however, economics are the driving force, with private developers and property owners worldwide wanting to make the most of their holdings. 'In every country there is a balance between private right and public interest', explains architectural historian Hiroyasu Fujioka. 'In Germany, public interest is more important but in Japan private interest is more important.' In Japan the owner usually has the last word.

One impetus for redevelopment is size. Due to improved building technology and changes to zoning laws it may be possible, as well as legally permissible, to build bigger than before. Architectural historian Hiroshi Matsukuma explains that this was partly due to the shift from timber to concrete construction that took place after World War II. Another reason was the 1963 revision to the clause in Japan's Building Standard law which capped the legal height limit at 31 metres (102 feet). Once that restriction was lifted, skyscrapers – starting with the Kasumigaseki Building in 1968 – began popping up. And owners, who were eager to use the fully permissible floor area, began replacing their smaller, existing buildings with new, bigger ones – an ongoing process that continues today.

Financial considerations also impact Japan's public facilities at the national, prefectural and municipal levels. Government agencies, which are routinely tasked with assessing whether renovation or rebuilding make better use of taxpayer money, often conclude that it is cheaper to demolish and start over. Plus, new construction is a better guarantee of public safety, which is a constant concern in an earthquake-prone country.

Since the 1950s, Japan has been coping with this threat by issuing increasingly stringent building codes after major earthquakes. These laws govern new construction but also apply to existing buildings that are subject to periodic inspections in the hope of averting their collapse during an earthquake. As few buildings, if any, are exempt from such review, 'grandfathering' a property is essentially not an option.

When a building fails to pass the test, the owner must pony-up to shore-up its structural system. 'Of course, reinforcement is possible, but it doesn't look nice and costs a lot', explains architect Taro Ashihara. In fact, the expense of retrofitting often rivals that of rebuilding altogether. In addition, the required changes can be so drastic that function is impaired or defunct entirely. When the Kagawa Prefectural Gymnasium, a ship-shaped masterpiece designed by Kenzo Tange in 1964, appeared unsound, reinforcing was an option. But the additional supports might prevent the building from serving as a gym. Caught in conundrums like this, local officials are confronted with the choice of using government funds to secure, repurpose and maintain an architecturally significant building or simply to take it down and rebuild. Whether an excuse or an explanation, seismic safety is frequently invoked as justification for demolition.

Kagawa Prefectural Gymnasium, Kenzo Tange, 1964.

Like Tange's gym, buildings erected in the 1950s and 1960s, when Japan's construction quality was lacking, can be especially vulnerable to destruction. 'After the war, the design skills were better than the construction capability', explains Shuko Koike, curator of architecture and culture. This was compounded by Japan's industrial growth and overall development that took off in the 1960s. As factories proliferated countrywide and individual car ownership spread, so did air pollution. This impacted building durability and, consequently, lifespan – even for structures made of concrete, a seemingly indestructible material.

Due to environmental damage, the life expectancy of reinforced concrete buildings fell from sixty to forty years according to architect Isao Hashimoto, whose firm, Maekawa Associates, used the material extensively. Hashimoto attributes this drop to the confluence of the inherent porosity of concrete and the increase of ambient carbon dioxide. By eroding exterior concrete surfaces, carbon dioxide enables rainwater to reach the internal steel structural scaffolding and cause it to rust. In turn, the accumulated rust causes the steel to expand and then the concrete to crack. 'People said "reinforced concrete doesn't work so let's take these buildings down"', comments Hashimoto. Maekawa's solution was not to abandon concrete construction altogether but to clad new works, such as the Tokyo Marine and Fire Insurance Building, with tile that shielded the concrete from the elements.

Tokyo Marine and Fire Insurance Building, Kunio Maekawa, 1974.

In addition to physical wear and tear, the passage of time can also lead to functional obsolescence. The failure to meet the changing needs of the population it serves can be the kiss of death for any building, but especially in Japan where there is generally less support for recycling architecture. Take the *kaikan*, or all-purpose community hall. As Japan rebuilt after the war, places where people could gather for cultural and other shared events sprang up in cities and towns up and down the archipelago. But, in due course, many of these large halls were deemed too generic, too big or too expensive to sustain, which led to their demolition.

Similarly, many of the dramatic buildings erected during the 'bubble economy' of the late 1980s had a particularly short shelf life. At this time, when money flowed very freely, appearance often trumped utility and

architectural one-upmanship became commonplace. Commercial clients with yen to burn commissioned Japanese and foreign designers alike for a variety of projects. Though these buildings had jobs to do, the primary purpose of many was to call attention to themselves (and implicitly their owners' businesses). 'It was design for design's sake', says Matsukuma. And, as Asahi Beer Hall exemplified, the bolder, the better.

Asahi Beer Hall, Philippe Starck, 1989.

Created by the French architect Philippe Starck, this striking building stands alone on the banks of Tokyo's Sumida River. An enigmatic, top-heavy structure covered in black stone and topped with a giant golden squiggle, it immediately garnered gobs of media attention and public curiosity when it opened in 1989. Numerous interpretations of its unique form circulated. However, though visible even from afar, few people had occasion to venture inside; that wasn't really the purpose.

While many of these bubble-era buildings were dismissed as folly and disregarded for their lack of functionality, they demonstrated the power of design to promote business and engage people on the street. In contrast to the stoic, clean lines of modern and even some post-modern predecessors, these loud, in-your-face structures were impossible to miss. Many soon fell prey to the wrecking ball, but before that they succeeded in raising the awareness of design and architecture for a general audience.

While the value of recent architecture remains underappreciated in Japan, historic buildings – temples, tearooms or even the red brick, Queen Anne-style Tokyo Station – are treasured. 'Why is one special and the other not?' probes Matsukuma. Undoubtedly, older buildings are receptacles of cultural heritage and are well known by the general population, thanks to textbooks and tourism. They are savoured for their enduring beauty, sense of craft and connection to the distant past. By contrast, newer buildings have yet to acquire that patina. 'It is difficult to appreciate concrete architecture in the same way', observes Ashihara.

This disparity also stems from the role of these revered buildings. Many are more ceremonial places that, unlike schools, shops and offices, are removed from practical, routine activity. 'Daily life buildings are not considered precious, so people do not care about them', explains architect Sou Fujimoto. Even those authored by talented designers often go unnoticed. And when roofs leak and floors do not have the depth to conceal computer cables, owners lose patience with these places.

'The value of a building should increase over time, but it's the opposite here [in Japan]', comments architect Tsuyoshi Tane. From the moment of a building's completion, its worth tends to decrease while the value of the land has historically grown in Japan's urban centres. Over time this disparity incentivizes rebuilding. If given the chance to stick around, perhaps some of these more recent buildings could also become important artefacts and acquire deeper cultural meaning. But this flies in the face of the country's love of the new, new thing.

The acquisition of the latest fashion, food, cars and other consumer goods is an endless and ongoing pursuit in Japan. Unquestionably, this appetite reflects the country's current wealth. Yet even in the 1960s, when the Japanese economy underwent huge growth and citizens gained disposable income, creature comforts were in great demand. Especially the so-called three 'sacred treasures': TV, refrigerator and washing machine. Nowadays, heated toilets, sophisticated air conditioning systems, mechanized locks and other high-tech devices have become de rigueur, and this too inspires replacing the old with the new.

Yet, when considered from a broader perspective, Japan's attachment to things of all sizes and shapes is fleeting. The belief that nothing material lasts forever – the concept of impermanence – is rooted in Buddhism. Though constructed from concrete and steel, buildings are not expected to stand indefinitely. This attitude is reinforced by the repeated episodes of mass destruction, natural as well as manmade, that have befallen Japan. Each time the country has regrouped and rebuilt, but it is always with the knowledge that another tragedy is bound to happen in the future.

Another expression of impermanence is the ancient custom of voluntary rebuilding. Made of wood components, the most famous example is Ise Shrine, whose innermost shrine – a simple timber structure blanketed with a thick, thatch roof – is painstakingly disassembled and recreated from identical but new parts on the adjacent site every twenty years, a process known as *Shikinen Sengu*. While the old wooden elements are dispersed to shrines around the country, new ones are crafted to the same specifications by highly specialized carpenters. By passing their skills onto the next generation of wood crafters, they enable the cycle to continue ad infinitum – and in so doing, preserve Japan's most venerated place of Shinto worship, albeit minus the building per se.

For secular structures, various types of recognition may be granted by government agencies at the national, prefectural and municipal levels. Yet these designations do not necessarily result in full-on preservation. In most cases the fate of even a publicly recognized building rests with its owner, and owners do not always welcome this status. On the one hand, receiving it may be beneficial and enable some government funding for upkeep. On the other, it may limit what can and cannot be done to the property. Even without government intervention, some owners choose to renovate or even repurpose. Sometimes converting existing buildings can be profitable. Plus, the cost of demolition can be very expensive.

Yet not all buildings can or deserve to be preserved. According to Professor Shin-ichi Okuyama of the Institute of Science Tokyo, the architect Kazuo Shinohara famously stated that European cities are so beautiful because they are frozen in time. By contrast, Tokyo, where time never stops, offers another kind of beauty. Indeed, commercial areas of Japanese cities, Tokyo chief among them, are places of thriving vitality. The steady infusion of new construction can promote life and activity. However, constant renewal comes at a cost. Once buildings come down, they are gone forever; we can no longer experience their inventiveness, elegance or sense of place. By at least preserving the memory of buildings, however, we can still savour their legacy and continue celebrating their glory.

Reader's notes: This book follows the Japanese/US convention of using 'first floor' to describe what in British English is termed 'ground floor'. Each profile includes dates of building completion and demolition. 'UNK' denotes where an exact demolition date is unknown; 'TBD' where demolition is planned, but with no fixed date yet determined.

Map of the Buildings

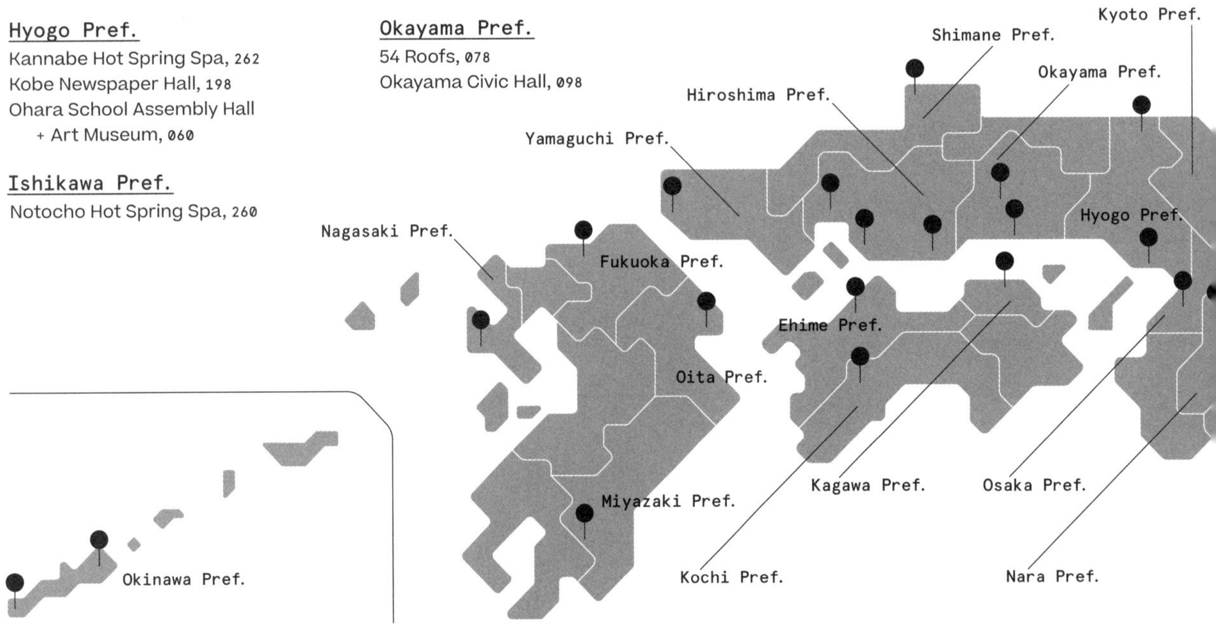

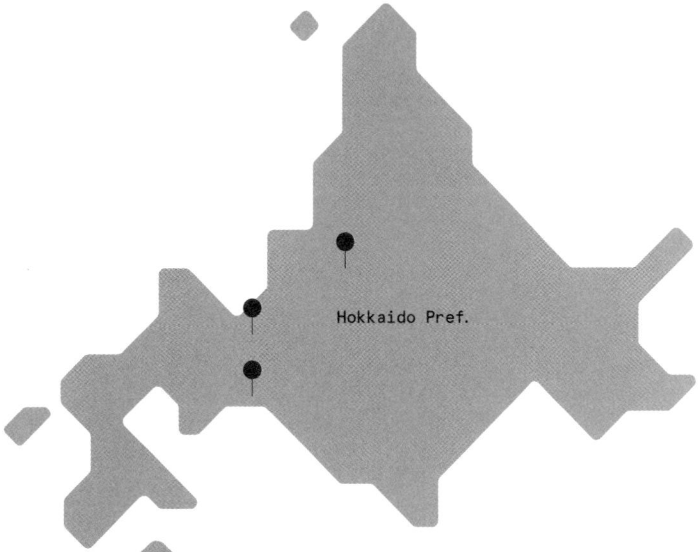
Hokkaido Pref.

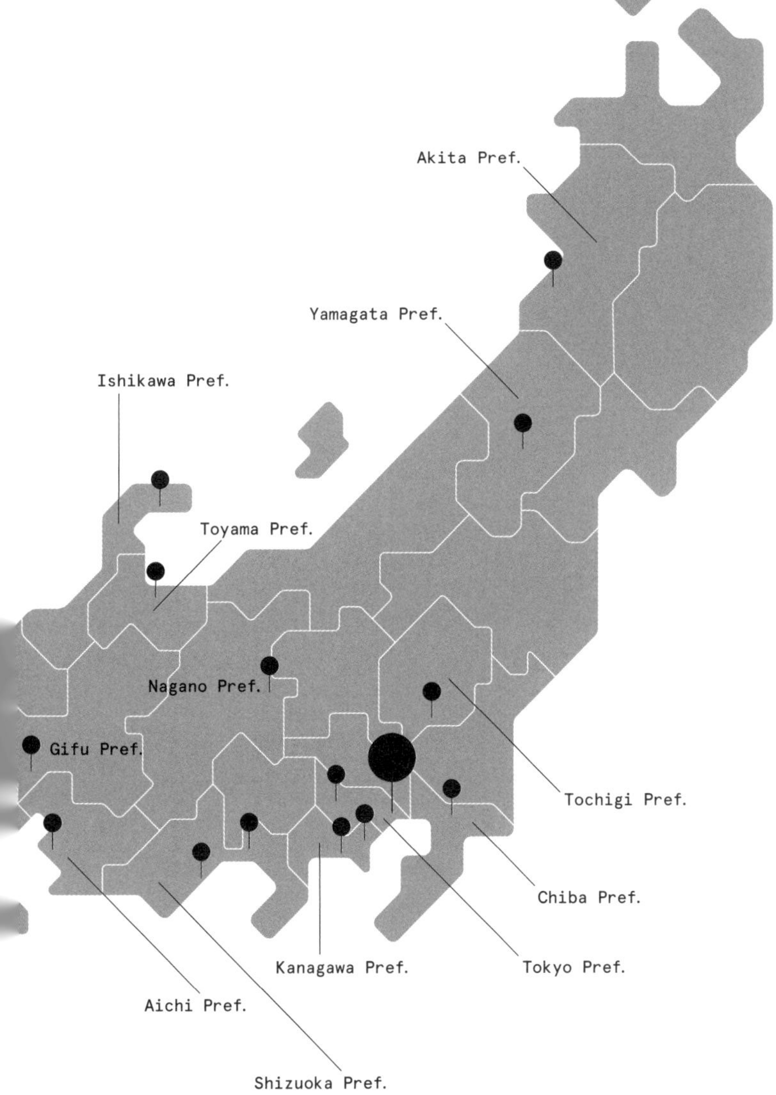
Akita Pref.
Yamagata Pref.
Ishikawa Pref.
Toyama Pref.
Nagano Pref.
Gifu Pref.
Tochigi Pref.
Chiba Pref.
Kanagawa Pref.
Tokyo Pref.
Aichi Pref.
Shizuoka Pref.

Tokyo Pref.

Consume

01

Eat
Drink
Imbibe
Buy
Purchase
Transact

Nippon Sogo Bank

In the aftermath of World War II, many Japanese architects wanted to weld tradition and Western Modernism. But Kunio Maekawa wanted to weld steel instead. With construction methodology as his guiding principle and prefabricated materials as his palette, Maekawa approached architectural design with measure and precision. 'He thought that only after learning technology could you design,' explains Isao Hashimoto, representative director at Maekawa Associates. One of Maekawa's first opportunities to test out his so-called 'technical approach' was with the headquarters of the Nippon Sogo Bank.

Located at a prominent intersection near Tokyo Station, the glass, steel and concrete edifice was a clean break from the ponderous masonry buildings nearby. 'Because of its relatively large size and its conspicuously new architectural style, the Sogo Bank marked a radical departure for the neighbourhood,' wrote historian Jonathan Reynolds.[3] This started at street level where hefty concrete columns gave the building the gravitas of a bank headquarters and enabled the double-height customer floor inside. For the office floors above and communal areas on top, Maekawa switched to a lighter-weight steel frame construction. This functional layering corresponded to the exterior's horizontal bands – the widest of all the curtainwall's syncopated windows covering the offices.

1952 –UNK

Architect: Kunio Maekawa
Location: Tokyo

Maruei Department Store

Unquestionably, the most dazzling feature of the Maruei Department Store was its west wall. An exuberant display of colour and eye-catching composition, the entire surface was done up with small squares of glass block and tile – red, blue, yellow, purple, brown, and most of all, green. Together they comprised a pastiche of abstract figures set against a green backdrop. With its muted tones and graceful designs, this mural-sized display may have been inspired by the intricate patterns of traditional kimono – no doubt a reference to Maruei's classic origin story.

Like many Japanese department stores, Maruei descended from a kimono purveyor founded in the Edo period (1603–1868). When this garment maker merged with another retailer in 1943, Maruei was born. Ten years later, Togo Murano, who already had department store designs under his belt, created its up-to-date emporium in downtown Nagoya.

Unlike many of his Modernist contemporaries, Murano wore applied ornament on his proverbial sleeve – the exterior wall was only the beginning. Inside, decorative flourish abounded. Lift doors featured fruit-bearing maidens; staircases incorporated delicate metalwork and bentwood rails. Luscious details like these underscored what a department store could be: a place of fantasy, a source of luxury and a break from the routine.

1953
2018

Architect: Togo Murano
Location: Aichi Prefecture

MARUEI
MARUEI
MARUEI
MARUEI
MARUEI
MARUEI
MARUEI
MARUEI
MARUEI
MARUEI
MARUEI
MARUEI
MARUEI

Café Printemps

Ebisubashi Branch
1965–late 1990s

Shinsaibashi Branch
1956–2004

Historically, neighbourhood parks, stores, restaurants and *sento* communal baths were functional extensions of the typically small Japanese home. Considered a private domain, the home was for family – socializing with others occurred elsewhere. In their day, Togo Murano's pair of Printemps cafés (no doubt named after the famous Ginza café meant to mimic its Parisian antecedents) were chic places to meet friends or simply take tea on one's own.

Constructed nine years apart, the two shops were operated by a historic plastering company, according to Murano archivist Ano Sato. An unusual arrangement, the company was not only Murano's client but also his contractor. Located in popular shopping areas, both cafés were sandwiched between buildings and fronted with double-height window walls. These artful compositions of glass rectangles and steel frames gave each one a presence on the street while revealing the inner workings: a street-level cashier counter and seating on the two upper floors.

But the likenesses stopped there. Adorned with ceramic tiles and Toulouse-Lautrec posters, the Shinsaibashi store had the flavour of an old-school European coffee house. By contrast, the all-white Ebisubashi outpost was resoundingly modern. From soup to nuts, its richly appointed interior – gracefully curving stairs, delicate pendant lights, rattan chairs and sculpted plaster ceiling – showcased Murano's exceptional taste for detail.

Architect: Togo Murano
Location: Osaka

(*top*) Ebisubashi branch.
(*bottom*) Shinsaibashi branch.

Fukuoka Sogo Bank

Oita Branch
1967–2007

Head Office
1971–UNK

Ropponmatsu Branch
1971–2012/13

Shortly after setting up his architectural practice, Arata Isozaki had a game-changing meeting with the president of the Fukuoka Sogo Bank. Though the newly minted architect only had one built work under his belt, the young bank executive made the bold move of commissioning him to design the bank's branch in Isozaki's hometown, Oita. What the banker sought was a fresh take on a stodgy building type. What he got was a sound investment. Over the next ten years, Isozaki went on to design several buildings for the bank – a major coup for the client and a phenomenal opportunity for an architect just starting out.

Turning tradition on its head, the top-heavy Oita branch featured a squat, stone-clad tower with sliced-off corners and few windows. Hovering three-stories above the ground, it was propped up by chunky columns. 'My intent at that time was to take a building – that is, an object overwhelmingly dominated by the force of gravity – and try to dematerialize it,' wrote Isozaki.[4] This bold strategy granted the building a distinctive presence that was visible from afar, while the low-scale banking hall hugging the ground welcomed customers with an entrance slanted towards the street – a taste of what awaited them inside. Devoid of right angles and boxy spaces, the double-height hall enabled customers to move freely as they went

Architect: Arata Isozaki
Locations: Oita Prefecture (Oita Branch); Fukuoka Prefecture (Head Office/Ropponmatsu Branch)

福岡相互銀行

about their business. This informal atmosphere was complemented by soft daylight entering from stripes of skylights and a profusion of colour: salmon pink walls and squiggly air-handling pipes painted bright red.

Having cut his teeth in Oita, Isozaki was next tasked with the bank's Fukuoka headquarters. This time the architect not only made a building but also an urban gesture. Covered in reddish-brown rock from India (where Isozaki had recently travelled), the flat, multistorey structure behaved like the backdrop for the expansive plaza in front of Hakata Station. At the same time, the plaza led up to Isozaki's edifice, which was fronted with a portico of beefy columns that supported a giant, granite-clad beam – perhaps references to the classic colonnaded façades of banks gone by.

If the Oita branch and Fukuoka headquarters played off history, the Ropponmatsu branch looked to the future. Like a streamlined machine, the entire bank was wrapped with squares of gleaming aluminium that rounded the building corners and were emblazoned on the street face with the words 'Home Bank' written in Lazenby Computer font.

(*p. 35*) Oita branch.
(*top*) Fukuoka headquarters.
(*opposite*) Ropponmatsu branch.

Kyoto Shinkin Bank, Shugakuin Branch

A stone's throw from the historic Shugakuin Imperial Villa, this was one of seventy branches Kiyonori Kikutake designed for the Kyoto Shinkin Bank. The architect is best known for his starring role in Japan's Metabolist design movement, which emerged in the 1960s. But in the 1950s, when new construction materials were scarce in the aftermath of World War II, Kikutake repurposed old ones such as steel signboard posts and timber beams. 'The reuse of materials was really important to the development of Kikutake's thinking', comments Professor Shingo Saito. And it dovetailed well with Metabolist buildings whose parts could be swapped – or metabolize – as needs changed. Case in point: this bank was composed of square units primed for future additions.

Perched at the intersection of two busy streets with a bus stop in front, the bank's four blocks were topped with hipped roofs held up by umbrella-shaped supports inside. More than an institutional entity, it had the appearance of a quaint village. And it functioned that way too. This wasn't only a place to tend to one's finances – the building incorporated a mini-community centre with places for kids to play and adults to gather.

1971
2021

Architect: Kiyonori Kikutake
Location: Kyoto

京都信用金
京都信用金庫専用駐車場
利用時間 平日 AM9:00～PM5:00
当金庫に御用のない方は、駐車ご遠慮下さい

Ingot Coffee Shop

Reminiscent of a greenhouse planted in the earth, the Ingot Coffee Shop was a simple shed covered entirely in glass. But, shaped like a parallelepiped, this was no ordinary shed. And coated with a mirror finish, this was no ordinary glass. Instead, its surface reflected the clouds, trees and sky during the day. Yet after the sun went down, the exterior wrapping all but melted away, revealing the shop's dreamy, otherworldly interior. Its conception demonstrated Shoei Yoh's love of light, which he manipulated like an architectural building block.

At this coffee shop, however, there really weren't many conventional building blocks. Devoid of columns, beams and walls, the café was essentially one big space. It had the atmosphere of a giant, light-filled sunroom with a bite taken out of the middle for the entrance. Here the white floor tiles flowed out like spilled milk, becoming the stepped exterior walkway. For the interior furnishings and fittings, Yoh stuck to the script with mirrored countertops, custom clear-glass tables and off-the-rack folding chairs – transparent of course. Though it wasn't envisioned as temporary, Yoh's embrace of light's ephemerality seemed to anticipate the shop's own demolition due to planned road widening.

1977
1986

Architect: Shoei Yoh
Location: Fukuoka Prefecture

Marufuji Minamidenen Grocery

When it comes to attention-grabbing buildings, the sky's the limit in Japan. Especially during the period of the country's soaring bubble economy, when Riken Yamamoto's career was also taking off. A favourite Yamamoto motif at that time was the tent-like roof panel. Made of lightweight punched metal or translucent plastic, these arched segments seem to lift his buildings skyward. While they served as sunshades at his own home, GAZEBO, in Yokohama, they became the signature motif of the Marufuji Minamidenen Grocery in Fussa.

A suburban community west of Tokyo, Fussa was better known for the United States air base nearby than cutting-edge architecture. But when Marufuji decided to upgrade its outpost here, the design-oriented Yamamoto was enlisted. Facing a busy throughfare, the building needed to capture motoring patrons as they zipped past. While the interior took its marching orders from the chain stores' template, the exterior was a blank slate. 'My goal was to make it conspicuous', explains the architect.

A billboard without being a billboard, Yamamoto's bold scheme initially surprised the client. But the stepped sequence of roofs landed well with shoppers. Due to the short shelf life of Japanese shops, the grocery was subsequently remodelled. Again. But a segment of Yamamoto's roof still hovers over the entrance today.

1986
–UNK

Architect: Riken Yamamoto
Location: Kanagawa Prefecture

MARUFUJI

Kirara Hikari Restaurant

In Japan, the typical udon noodle joint has a *noren* curtain above its doorway, rustic wood panelling lining its walls and assorted other features tied to tradition. But Kirara Hikari, Riken Yamamoto's prototype for an up-to-date udon shop chain, made a clean break from the past. Situated far from the local train station, amid a roadside restaurant strip at the edge of Tokyo, it had to attract customers driving past. Riken Yamamoto knew that he could whet their appetites by serving up a shop that was fresh, transparent and, above all, modern.

But familiarity was also an essential ingredient. Combining old and new, Yamamoto tapped an architectural icon and topped the restaurant with an expansive pitched roof. This dramatic form, which reached a whopping eight metres (twenty-six feet) at its apex, evoked the traditional *minka* farmhouses that still exist countrywide. Yet, instead of bulky wooden beams and columns, and a thick blanket of thatch, Yamamoto favoured lightweight steel ribs covered with wafer-thin plastic panels. There was no need for garish signage – the building spoke for itself, especially after the sun went down and its translucent wrapping glowed like a super-sized *andon* lantern. 'It was visible from far away, even at night', reminisced Yamamoto.

1986 –UNK

Architect: Riken Yamamoto
Location: Tokyo

DEEP DIVE

Japanese Preservation Laws in a Nutshell

Created for the 1964 Tokyo Olympics, Kenzo Tange's Yoyogi National Gymnasium is among the most impactful buildings ever constructed in Japan. A magnificent feat of architecture and engineering, its energetic swirling roof was not only the perfect metaphor for athletic competition, but also presented the country's newfound technical might to the entire world. Though its swimming pools are no longer regulation size, the gymnasium was designated by the Japanese Government as an Important Cultural Property in 2021 – an honour that assured the building's longevity.

But the treatment of this gym is the exception. For the most part, post-World War II buildings are unprotected, though the concept of preservation has existed since the Meiji era (1868–1912). At that time, measures were taken to fund shrines and temples previously supported by the newly demoted warrior ruling class. In 1929, the National Treasures Preservation Law instituted the National Treasure system that singles out people, places and objects of cultural importance. And coverage was broadened considerably more in 1950 with the introduction of the Act for the Protection of Cultural Properties – Japan's first comprehensive legal framework for protecting cultural assets.

Under the aegis of the Agency for Cultural Affairs, this sweeping legislation preserves and protects both intangibles, such as drama and music, and tangibles, such as artworks, crafts and gardens plus historic castles, teahouses, residences and the like. Though the criteria are somewhat subjective, the goal is to elevate and esteem Japan's cultural assets by designating them as Important Cultural Properties or National Treasures. In the case of buildings, this recognition limits demolition and requires approval for even minor changes. But it also provides extensive government funding for repairs.

By the 1980s, protection spread to Meiji-era red brick, Western-style buildings. And the Registration system instituted in 1996 made preservation even more widely attainable. Most buildings that are fifty years old can be registered, explains Kazuhiko Nishi of the Agency for Cultural Affairs. While its requirements and restrictions are far less stringent than those of the Designation system, the decision whether to demolish or not belongs to the owner.

For some property holders, a Registered building is a source of pride and can even be income generating – the official plaque can lure customers to their rice cracker shops and *ryokan* inns – but owners bear the lion's share of conservation costs. For this reason and others, some choose not to register their buildings or later de-list and dismantle them instead.

No doubt the government cultural recognition programmes have helped raise public awareness of the value of architecture. But for post-war buildings there is a long way to go. 'They're like a species of bird in danger of extinction', said architectural historian Hiroshi Matsukuma.[5] Some will survive, but many will not.

(*opposite*) Yoyogi National Gymnasium, Kenzo Tange, 1964.

Learn

02

Study
Discover
Comprehend
Observe
Understand
Absorb

Hiroshima Children's Library

When it comes to Japanese cities, none carry the weight of Hiroshima. Decimated by an Allied atomic bomb in 1945, the city was largely levelled, and the loss of life was catastrophic. This event was commemorated by the Hiroshima Peace Memorial Park, the competition-winning commission that established Kenzo Tange's career. His elegant scheme created a place for mourning, as well as a place to hope for peace, in a park-like setting. Suitably, it was on these grounds that his Children's Library also once stood.

A modest circular building encased with glass, the building was essentially one big room divided by free-standing bookshelves with clusters of kid-sized tables and chairs in between. But the most striking feature was its complete integration of architecture and structure – it was hard to say where one ended and the other began. This was Tange's first collaboration with engineer Yoshikatsu Tsuboi, with whom he went on to design, among other things, the Yoyogi National Gymnasium for the 1964 Tokyo Olympics. Rising from the centre of the library, the trunk-like concrete core branched out into a shallow bowl supporting the roof. Both a structural innovation and a symbolic gesture, this was a sunny, welcoming place where growing kids could stretch their imaginations.

1953
1978

Architect: Kenzo Tange
Location: Hiroshima Prefecture

Kaisei Senior High School + Kureha Junior High School

Kaisei Senior
High School
1959–2015

Kureha Junior
High School
1958–2005

Though designed in close succession, these two schools were practically polar opposites. One was in the south and the other in the north. One was sited on flat terrain and the other on a steep slope. And one stood up straight while the other spread out. Popular with their students, they both underscored the architect's talent for making places where kids wanted to be and could learn.

First came Kaisei Senior High School, which occupied a hillside plot overlooking Nagasaki, the Kyushu city famous for its early embrace of Christianity as well as its annihilation by the second Allied atomic bomb. 'After the [Pacific] War, new things were considered good things', comments former Yosizaka staff member, Yuko Saito. Breaking from the past, Yosizaka's six-storey school bore the distinct imprint of his mentor, the Swiss architect Le Corbusier. Evoking his brand of Modernism, Yosizaka used concrete to create angled exterior walls and a cylindrical stair tower peppered with tiny windows. Crowned with a statue of the Virgin Mary, the tower had a commanding, visible, presence amid the surrounding area.

By contrast, the Kureha Junior High School reached out into the landscape with three Y-shaped buildings that encircled a courtyard. While bridges linked the buildings, exterior corridors connected the classrooms. This standard feature of Japanese public schools doubled as impromptu balconies where kids happily hung out.

Architect: Takamasa Yosizaka + Atelier U
Locations: Nagasaki Prefecture (Kaisei),
Toyama Prefecture (Kureha)

(*top*) Kaisei Senior High School.
(*overleaf*) Kureha Junior High School.

Ohara School Assembly Hall + Art Museum

Assembly Hall
1962–2025

Art Museum
1970–2025

Among Japan's most enduring art forms is *ikebana* flower arranging. One of the more than three hundred different organizations promoting the beauty of blooms and providing instruction in how to position them, the Ohara School began in 1895. It was the founder's grandson and successor as headmaster, Houn Ohara, who commissioned Kiyoshi Seike to create four buildings in just ten years for the school's Kobe headquarters. A dream commission if ever there was one! Especially for Seike who was often inspired by the landscape. Embedded in the hillside site, Seike's buildings grew directly from the ground.

The first of the four projects was the Assembly Hall housing the school's office, gallery, classrooms, student lodgings and an atelier for Ohara. While the base of the oblong building consisted of granite boulders excavated on the property, the roof had a distinctive wavy profile. Its deep eaves cast scalloped shadows on the façade, which was composed of ornamental ceramic blocks. Using similar building blocks, the three-storey Art Museum, the fourth and final addition to the complex (which also included Ohara's home and the school's Memorial Hall), held a string of single- and double-height spaces where Ohara's collection of primitives and other artworks could inspire students.

Architect: Kiyoshi Seike
Location: Hyogo Prefecture

(*opposite*) Art Museum.
(*overleaf*) Assembly Hall.

Keisho Kindergarten

The Keisho Kindergarten must have been a delightful place to start school – even Hiroshi Hara's own son and daughter were enrolled. Of course, its mission was early learning, but its modus operandum was fun.

No doubt the architect's firsthand experience with young children informed his long, skinny building that began with a giant outdoor stair directly opposite the school's front gate. It ascended to a rooftop play area where an individual staircase descended to each classroom – how nifty is that? More like glorified alcoves, these teaching areas flowed into a generous corridor culminating in the communal double-height playroom where the ceiling tilted upward, as if balancing the exterior stairs at the other end.

Another enchantment was the exuberant use of colour. 'I wanted to create the interior of the building like clothing', explained Hara.[6] While every room wore a different shade, the corridor was adorned with stripes and the playroom was a patchwork of oranges and yellows. Bursting with energy, all the kids' spaces spilled out onto the ground-level playground. Here, young imaginations could run wild under the watchful eyes of the teachers perched in the staff room jutting out above.

1968
–UNK

Architect: Hiroshi Hara
Location: Tokyo

慶松幼稚園

Mount Ikoma Space Science Pavilion

Perched amid a mountaintop amusement park, this space museum bore a closer resemblance to an alien UFO than a learning centre. As if poised for take-off, its oval drum of a building was capped by a tilted roof angled towards the sky but weighted down by a giant trough-shaped beam. On rainy days, this concrete conduit guided rivulets of water down to a shallow pool in front of the pavilion. Yet on sunny days, it directed the eye and, implicitly, the imagination upward towards outer space. 'It was like the symbol of the building,' recalls former Yosizaka staff member, Yuko Saito.

Unsurprisingly, rockets, planets and distant galaxies were on everyone's mind when this project was completed. The United States had landed on the moon the year before and Japan's own futuristic Expo '70 was underway in nearby Osaka. Spaceship models and related artefacts dominated the exhibition area – a scaleless place with a soaring ceiling. This colossal space orbited around a single towering column which supported the trough outside and spoke-like steel trusses inside. A room-within-a-room, the domed planetarium was Yosizaka's only concession to convention. 'He really wanted to make a different world,' comments Saito.

1970
2015

Architect: Takamasa Yosizaka + Atelier U
Location: Nara Prefecture

生駒山宇宙科学館

St. Mary's International School

In contrast to Japan's standard-issue public schools, this building was conceived as 'a landscape for children', in the words of architect and Pritzker Prize winner Fumihiko Maki.[7] A private Catholic institution for boys founded in 1954, St. Mary's catered to the foreign community. Consequently, the school's mission was independent of the Ministry of Education's rigid pedagogy and concomitant physical requirements, such as sinks, so the kids could clean the building, and unicycle storage for their de rigueur daily exercise. In 1971, Maki's enticing idea came to life when St. Mary's moved to its leafy campus in western Tokyo.

A lovely blend of the manmade and the natural, Maki's school was set back from the street by a large lawn. Behind its façade, a long circulation spine contained assorted administrative functions and spawned wings for classrooms, cafeteria and athletics facilities. Extending out into the grassy terrain, these appendages were configured to protect the site's majestic trees while enclosing a courtyard where the young lads could play and explore. They also yielded the building's many exterior walls, which Maki dotted with windows up high and down low, bathing the corridors and classrooms with soft daylight. 'It was magical, warm and comforting, bringing to the children inside a sense of security and gentleness', recalls gallerist and St. Mary's alum, Wahei Aoyama.

1970
2010

Architect: Fumihiko Maki
Location: Tokyo

PEPSI

Honjo Kindergarten

Having designed more than five *hoikuen* kindergartens, Kinya Maruyama knows his way around tot-friendly spaces. In addition to the practical places for eating, napping and toileting, the young charges require plenty of room to play, learn and, above all, have fun. 'I try to think about kids' physical abilities as well as their imagination', explains the architect.

Intended to aid working parents, the typical *hoikuen* offers all-day care for infants to five-year-olds. But many have been forced to close due to the country's declining birthrate. In its heyday, however, the Honjo Kindergarten could accommodate up to 150 kids at once. Spread out over two stories, the building held separate areas for different activities and ages. These places were unified by wide stairs, interior windows and unexpected wall openings – each element an invitation to climb, run, jump or just sit quietly while listening to a story.

Yet one of the building's most playful features was outside. 'Very often children are drawn to the shape of the roof', explains Maruyama. In the case of Honjo, its swoopy planes surmounted with a bird-shaped weathervane hinted at the child-friendly world inside.

1975 –UNK

Architects: Kinya Maruyama / Atelier Mobile / Team Zoo
Location: Akita Prefecture

National Aquarium, Okinawa

The southernmost tip of the Japanese archipelago, Okinawa is a subtropical island where the sun is strong, the skies are blue, and the fish are plentiful. Constructed at the time of the International Ocean Expo of 1975, this National Aquarium celebrated local sea creatures of various sorts. 'One might see it as an art museum of fish', wrote architect Fumihiko Maki.[8] Instead of the usual string of small, boxy displays, Maki's main events were two giant tanks for coral sea and deep-sea critters respectively. These were integrated with carpeted seating areas where visitors could sit back and watch the fish frolicking while listening to piped-in electronic music.

The facility was encased in an L-shaped concrete shell of a building composed of arches piled on top of arches, ziggurat-style. Curbing the intense sun, the curved openings formed the covered approach to the main entrance as well as an ocean-facing promenade. As the sun shifted position throughout the day, the arches created an ever-changing play of light and shadow on the building's concrete exterior. Painted brown to match the island's local brick, Maki's building was completely at home in the Okinawan landscape.

1975
2002

Architect: Fumihiko Maki
Location: Okinawa

54 Roofs

In Japan, fifty-four is not just any old number. There were fifty-four post stations on the historic Tokkaido highway between Kyoto and Edo (as Tokyo was known until 1868). There were fifty-four chapters in the 11th-century literary classic, *The Tale of Genji*. And twice the amount, 108, is the number of stitches on a baseball – essential equipment for one of Japan's favourite pastimes. Perhaps these associations explain why the number also made numerous appearances in the work of Kazuhiro Ishii, such as the private home, 54 Windows, in Kanagawa Prefecture and the wedding hall, 54 Columns, in Saitama Prefecture.

Located in the tranquil countryside of Okayama Prefecture, 54 Roofs – a kindergarten – was defined by fifty-four pointy-topped frames. Uniting the building with its surroundings, the roofs' saw-toothed profile seemed to be in dialogue with the hilly landscape in the distance. This cluster of pitched-roof forms – the universal symbol of a house, legible to kids worldwide – resembled a manmade mini-village. At the building's perimeter, they stood shoulder to shoulder like a picket fence. But inside they formed playful, tot-sized spaces that invited the imagination and were surely etched in the memories of the youngsters schooled here.

1979
2009

Architect: Kazuhiro Ishii
Location: Okayama Prefecture

Cunningham Harmony House

Developed during the 19th century as a retreat from Tokyo's scorching summers, Karuizawa began as a charming village with lovely country homes and a lively shopping street for stocking the larder. It was here that Junzo Yoshimura built his own second home in 1963. And it was here that his client, Eloise Cunningham, a missionary daughter who grew up in Japan, decided to create a place for children to make music. Having attended the Oberlin Conservatory of Music in Ohio, Cunningham was aware of the many music camps available to kids in the United States and was keen to create such a centre in Japan.

Sharing connections to both Karuizawa and music, Yoshimura – who had already designed performance and practice spaces – was completely in tune with his client's vision. The L-shaped building he composed featured living quarters in one wing and a communal practice and performance space in the other. From here, gentle ramps led up to an informal stage or down to the dining room and sliding window walls opened to the greenery outside. 'It was such a congenial place', recalls Yoshimura's daughter, Takako, who runs a separate music school founded by her mother. 'Young children not only learned music, but how to live together.'

1983
2024

Architect: Junzo Yoshimura
Location: Nagano Prefecture

Tsuda Hall

Dedicated to the education of women, Tsuda College was the brainchild of Umeko Tsuda, who founded the school in 1900. At the age of six, she was among the first Japanese girls to have been educated in the United States, an experience that laid the groundwork for the university that now bears her name. Tsuda Hall, the cornerstone of the school's satellite central Tokyo campus, was designed by Fumihiko Maki, himself an important architectural bridge between Japan and America.

Standing at a busy intersection, Tsuda Hall faced both Sendagaya Station and the Tokyo Metropolitan Gymnasium, also designed by Maki. An exercise in what Maki termed 'collective form', it collaged individual sports facilities in a park-like setting. Though separated by the street, Tsuda Hall was like an extension of this athletics campus.

Compared to the muscly main arena with its large metal roof, Tsuda Hall was small potatoes. But in the life of the school, it was a valued team player. Containing lecture, conference and concert halls, it faced the street with an array of geometric windows – squares, rectangles and one big triangle marking the corner. Yet, despite his love of straight lines, Maki didn't shy away from curves. Instead, Tsuda Hall crescendoed in a dramatic arch that covered the top-floor auditorium and created its distinct identity.

1988
2018

Architect: Fumihiko Maki
Location: Tokyo

Govern

03

Oversee
Manage
Guide
Lead
Supervise
Administer

Ehime Prefectural Hall

After the destruction wrought by World War II, Japan urgently needed tons of new buildings – big and small, public and private. Yet construction supplies and labour, not to mention financing, were very limited. In fact, when it came to this building, Kenzo Tange was asked to reuse an existing airplane hangar's structural steel frames as a budget-saving measure. But the architect opted for concrete. Relatively cheap, readily available and unquestionably malleable, the material offered a wealth of possibilities. Especially in the hands of Tange and his collaborating engineer, Yoshikatsu Tsuboi.

The team created a shallow shell for the roof which enabled a large, column-free arena below. In Tange's words, it was like a crab's hard exoskeleton.[9] Dotted with tiny, twinkling skylights, the spherical surface tilted upward above the stepped tiers of spectator seating. Both roof and elevated chairs were propped up from below by a ring of hulking piers that stood outside. Despite its ponderous concrete construction, the dynamism of Tange's architecture must have been palpable. Though built in celebration of the National Sports Festival, the hall went on to host concerts and other crowd-pleasing events.

1953
1996

Architect: Kenzo Tange
Location: Ehime Prefecture

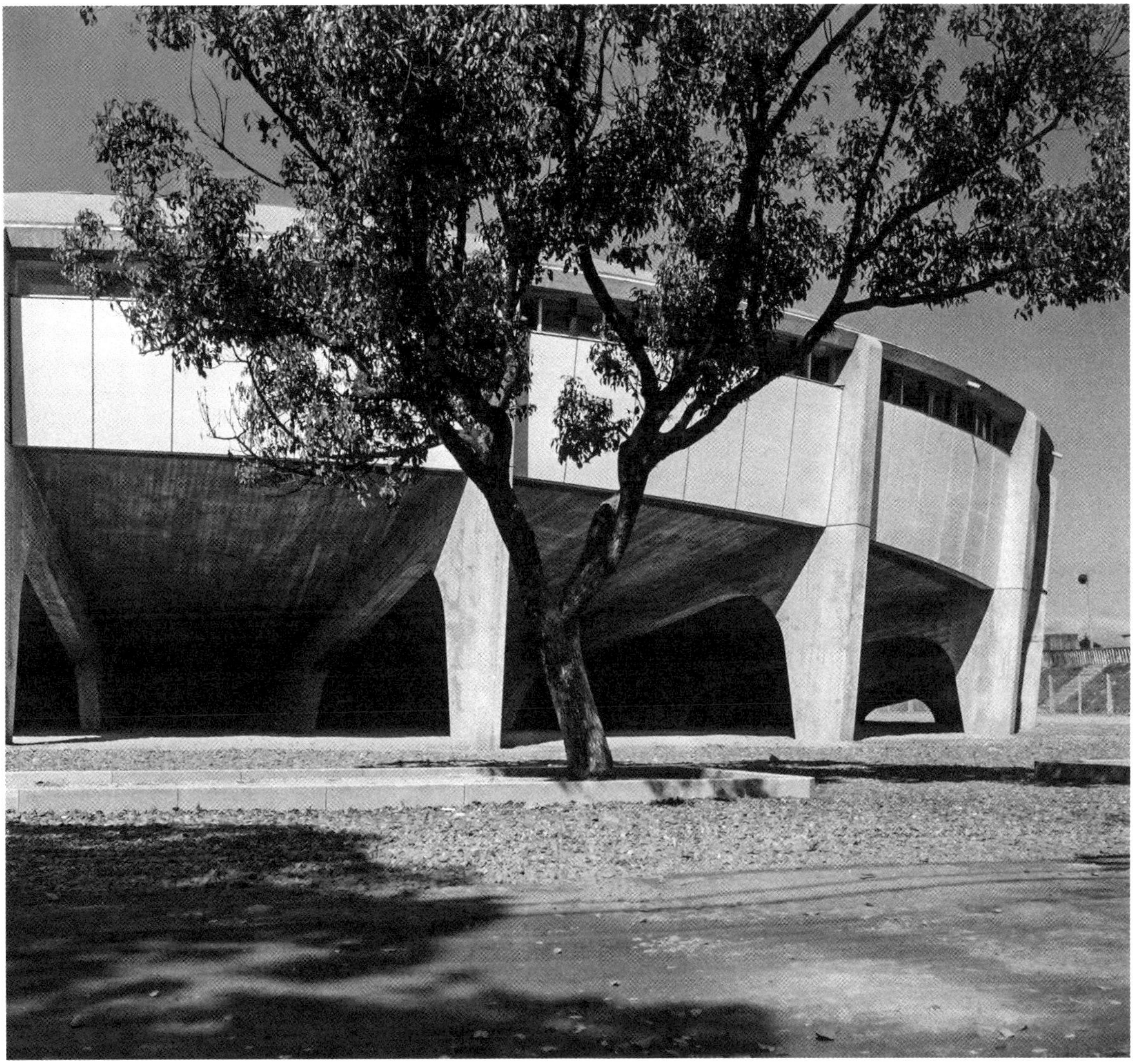

Tokyo Metropolitan Government Office

In 1952, a competition was held for the new Tokyo Metropolitan Government Office. It was slated for a site in Yurakucho where a steady stream of commuters and business executives pass daily. Kenzo Tange, the architect of the much-applauded Hiroshima Peace Memorial, took first prize. Instead of being put off by the area's bustle, he embraced this chance to make a citizen-forward city hall at Tokyo's core. 'Each individual building must be considered to be an important element of the urban plan', wrote Tange.[10] Here, that took the form of an eight-storey edifice whose height fitted within the legally permissible 31 metres (102 feet), and whose open base interacted with the public.

Tange connected his building to the city with a two-tiered access system. While cars circulated or parked at street level, people moved about on an open mezzanine wrapping the building perimeter above. The two were connected by short runs of stairs and *piloti* columns – the defining feature of the pedestrian zone. 'His idea was to create an open area (*piloti* space) ... to catch the horizontal flow of people that arrived from all across the Kanto region each morning', explains architectural historian Saikaku Toyokawa.[11]

Above the mezzanine, the building was enclosed with deep-set glass walls screened by a louvred grid that passively controlled sunlight and heat gain. 'This has the same effect as Japanese houses with deep eaves', explained Tange.[12]

1957
1991

Architect: Kenzo Tange
Location: Tokyo

3rd ASIAN GAMES

The choice of glass may have reflected the growing use of curtainwall by Modernists like Mies van der Rohe. But it also related to traditional Japanese buildings whose sliding exterior screens were barely walls at all according to critic Noboru Kawazoe: 'For the Western architect, glass is considered a surface wall, but for the Japanese architect it is a kind of transparent nothingness'.[13]

In part, the glass enclosure was enabled by the building core which provided structural support and incorporated a variety of vertical elements, including stairs, lifts, ducts and piping. '[The core] stands sturdily much like the trunk of a tree', observed Tange.[14] This strategy also yielded plenty of open interior space – the ground-floor lobby the most impressive of all. This grand, two-storey entrance was furnished with sculptural stools and benches plus a colossal ceramic wall piece by the artist Taro Okamoto. Recalls the architect's daughter, Michiko Uchida: 'I was only a child of seven or eight, but the mural was so impressive.'

Asahikawa City Hall

Hokkaido, Japan's northernmost island, is famous for its snow. It is also known for brick buildings. Developed during the Meiji era (1868–1912), the red masonry of these structures stands up to the bone-chilling cold and stands out against the mountainous white drifts that accumulate each winter. Born and partially bred in Hokkaido, Takeo Satow was inspired by both attributes when he designed the City Hall for Asahikawa, the island's second largest city.

Satow's scheme consisted of two main parts: high-rise offices ringed by the low-rise base that incorporated a variety of citizen services and legislative activities, including the parliament hall whose dramatic roof popped up above the building. 'Satow's pattern was to place a tower on flat land', explains Koichi Yumizaki of AXS Satow Inc. This composition contrasted sharply with the small, pitched-roof buildings nearby. So did Satow's concrete construction. Yet his red brick inlays also nodded to Hokkaido's rich architectural history.

'Satow cared deeply about making good civic spaces', comments Mayumi Takahashi of AXS Satow. He achieved this with abundant windows, a courtyard garden and clean geometry that limited snow build-up at the base. An exterior-mounted clock – a recurrent Satow motif – contributed to the building's identity. 'People could see it from everywhere', recalls Yumizaki.

1958
2024

Architect: Takeo Satow
Location: Hokkaido

Hashima City Hall

Over the course of his prolific career, Junzo Sakakura designed a wide range of public and private buildings throughout Japan. Created for his hometown, this building was surely dear to his heart. The son of the thirteenth head of his family's sake brewery located in the centre of Hashima, Sakakura had deep roots here and visited frequently. Just a stone's throw from the architect's birthplace, Hashima's City Hall blended Sakakura's Modernist design sensibility with his intimate understanding of the site.

Surrounded by low houses, rice paddies and lotus ponds, Sakakura's concrete edifice stood out but also offered magnificent views of the idyllic landscape and majestic Mount Ibuki in the distance. Evoking the work of the Swiss architect and Sakakura mentor, Le Corbusier, the building's second-floor main entrance was accessed by three exterior ramps intended to welcome citizens coming from various parts of the city. Inside was a variety of municipal and public amenities, including the city council chamber and community hall poking up from the roof – the latter enclosed with a concave concrete shell and the former convex – which gave City Hall its distinctive profile.

1959
2024

Architect: Junzo Sakakura
Location: Gifu Prefecture

Kure City Hall + Civic Centre

This pair stood in the centre of Kure, an active port and shipbuilding city facing the Seto Inland Sea. Surrounded by nine hilly peaks, Kure was home to a major naval base during World War II and, consequently, became a target of Allied firebombs. The widespread destruction ultimately gave rise to the construction of the new City Hall and Civic Centre.

Like ship funnels writ large, giant cones figured prominently in the complex. At the Civic Centre this took the form of two wraparound wall segments encircling the theatre. According to the architect and Junzo Sakakura archivist, Noribumi Kitamura, whose father was a member of the firm's Civic Centre design team, the theatre started out as a straight-up cylinder that was flattened to create the building's splayed shape. This manipulation yielded a gap between the façade and the ground – the ideal spot for the glass-enclosed foyer and main entrance. The other cone held the city council's assembly hall, next door to the government's rectangular office mini tower.

The entire development was tied together by a network of elevated plazas and walkways separating pedestrians from the car traffic below. Materials were another shared feature: earthy, exposed concrete and gleaming, marine-blue tiles covering the cones.

1962
2016

Architect: Junzo Sakakura
Location: Hiroshima Prefecture

Okayama Civic Hall

The Okayama Civic Hall was an architectural statement and an urban gesture all in one. Together with its doppelganger, Takeo Satow's Sanyo Broadcasting Hall, it framed an open plaza for public gatherings while inside it accommodated get-togethers large and small – a much-needed resource after the war.

'At that time there were few venues to hold weddings, so the local government often provided such facilities', explains Koichi Yumizaki of AXS Satow Inc. Not to mention places for concerts, plays, lectures and other performing arts. Satow responded with a two-part building. Facing the plaza, its opening act was a rectangular box that held smaller halls and was covered with concrete tracery. But the star of the show was the 1,761-seat octagonal auditorium beyond.

Outside, the hall's geometry was defined by faceted wall segments interspersed with stained-glass panels. While the solid sections were clad with red-brown clay tiles evoking the prefecture's famous Bizen ceramics, the colourful glass blocks animated the foyer inside. A fan of artistic collaborations, Satow enlisted the designer Katsuki Iwabuchi to devise the glasswork. For the foyer's backdrop, he invited the abstract painter Kenji Yoshida, who created *FAUN*, a large relief carved directly into the concrete. Throughout the building, textured concrete surfaces added dramatic flair while benefitting the auditorium's acoustics.

1963
2024

Architect: Takeo Satow
Location: Okayama Prefecture

Miyakonojo Civic Centre

This building came out of the ground when the construction of the *kaikan*, or multipurpose civic hall, was all the rage. Ravaged by World War II, many communities had no place where citizens could gather for large cultural events or even small group meetings. Consequently, towns and cities up and down the archipelago – including the far reaches of Kyushu island's Miyazaki Prefecture – jumped on the bandwagon and built one of their own.

Over time, these buildings ceased to serve their public. Concerts needed better acoustics, auditoria needed more seats, and theatres needed bigger stages. In short, multipurpose had no purpose. Rising maintenance costs (funded by taxpayers) coupled with dwindling populations, especially in the hinterlands, also sounded the *kaikan*'s death knell. Sadly, these reasons and others led to the demise of many of these architectural gems. Chief among the casualties was Kiyonori Kikutake's exceptional Miyakonojo Civic Centre.

Despite its complicated presentation, Kikutake's hall consisted of two principal and distinct parts: a concrete base, containing a rabbit's warren of meeting rooms and other subsidiary spaces, and the theatre with its dynamic, dramatic roof. Created with great C-shaped ribs, steel plates and tension rods, this show-stopping shape fanned out like the hood of a classic Silver Cross pram – it even looked as if it could be opened or closed. Inherent in the roof's assembly was

1969
2019

Architect: Kiyonori Kikutake
Location: Miyazaki Prefecture

the possibility of swapping out bits and pieces should they need repair or reconfiguring. This organic idea was in keeping with Kikutake's embrace of Metabolism, Japan's homegrown design movement that promoted architecture with built-in changeability.

In contrast to the roof's potential for replacement parts, the rock-solid rectangular building bottom was immutable. One end held the centre's porticoed street-level entrance located below the theatre's angled underbelly, which was propped up by concrete columns. The other was topped with an outdoor stage that backed onto the outer wall of the main theatre. Inside, the theatre's arched ceiling echoed the roof's distinctive profile as it swooped up above the descending rows of seating and directed the eye towards the proscenium stage.

Unquestionably, this Civic Centre contrasted strongly with all other buildings in the vicinity or, for that matter, anywhere. There really was nothing like it. This was a fantastic, futuristic structure that had the power to transport people not just with the performances produced inside but through Kikutake's bold vision of what a *kaikan* could be.

Naha Civic Hall

Climate and construction often go hand in hand. Especially in Okinawa, the subtropical island at the tail of the Japanese archipelago. Think blistering sun, blustery typhoons and relentless heat. Buffered from the elements with wraparound, tile-clad *amahaji* eaves, this building combined international Modernism with the Okinawan vernacular – a concern near and dear to its architect, Nobuyoshi. Threatened by World War II damage followed by the United States occupation, Indigenous traditions were at risk of disappearing.

Intended for plays, concerts and other performing arts, the low-slung, two-storey building was the island's first major community centre built according to Masaru Kinjo, the architect's architect son. Approached from the street, its wide stairs ascended to the louvred promenade that cut through the building's second floor. Flanking this semi-outdoor corridor were two theatres, with offices and meetings rooms downstairs. Keeping local customs alive, a partial height *hinpun* stone screen, the historic device for shielding homes from passersby, partitioned the entry foyer and lounge. But the building's main claim to fame was its hosting of Okinawa's celebration of the island's return to Japanese sovereignty in 1972.

1970
2024

Architects: Nobuyoshi Kinjo + Gendai Sekkei Co., Ltd.
Location: Okinawa

Asacho Agricultural Centre

There is something meta about a community centre modelled after the centre of a community. The main gathering place for a small agricultural cooperative, this building was a townscape in miniature. It featured a circular multipurpose hall (for weddings, performances and other group activities) that was ringed by assorted support spaces, each one housed in its own organically shaped volume. Like mini buildings, they deftly negotiated the hall's pure geometry with the land's lumps and bumps.

Poking up from the town's patchwork of pitched-roof houses, the big hall was topped with a dome – a common sight in European and American cities but a rarity Japan. Yet the round roof was not entirely out of place since it acknowledged the gently sloping peaks off in the distance. 'Essentially we made another mountain,' explains Team Zoo principal, Reiko Tomita.

Another contextual cue was the building's vernacular clay tile roof. The red-brown shingles covered the dome as well as the triangular dormers jutting out in every direction. In keeping with Japan's tradition of rooftop talismans, each opening was capped with one of the twelve animals of the Asian zodiac or another protective motif.

1985
2002

Architects: Reiko Tomita / Atelier Zo / Team Zoo
Location: Hiroshima Prefecture

Higashinihonbashi Police Box

Unquestionably, this was not your typical police box. Unsurprisingly, it came about when the National Police Agency decided to soften their image by commissioning architects to create some of these neighbourhood outposts. In choosing Atsushi Kitagawara, they more than met their goal.

'I wanted to design a friendly *koban* [police box]', explains Kitagawara. 'A police officer should be someone you'd like to talk to'. With its attention-grabbing form and welcoming demeanour, Kitagawara's two-part mini building – one half concrete and the other metal mesh – attracted visitors from multiple directions. Inside, it held the standard consultation room for public and police interface plus a private kitchen, tatami-floored rest area, holding room for perpetrators, and weapons storage for officers only.

This bold little building stood sentry on a small, triangular plot at the intersection of five roads – a key node amid a once thriving wholesale district. Acknowledging this past, the concrete's rectilinear geometry recalled the rows of wooden buildings that once lined the nearby streets. Abstract representations of the colourful bustle of commercial activity, red, blue and yellow pieces were held by the concrete. By contrast, the enigmatic, shimmery shape pointed towards the future. 'No one knows what the future will bring', explains the architect. Sadly, it brought the road-widening that took down this gem.

1992
2001

Architect: Atsushi Kitagawara
Location: Tokyo

HOBBY
CRAFT
marbee7

Chofu Police Box

Unquestionably Tokyo is one of the safest cities in the world. Perhaps the prevalence of neighbourhood police boxes is one reason. Points of daily contact with the community, these tiny, two- to three-person outposts quietly surveil their surroundings while fielding questions from passersby. Keen to make their officers even more approachable, the National Police Agency began inviting newly minted architects in 1983 to design police boxes. Aside from functional requirements, which included places for public interface, and private work and sleeping areas for officers on overnight shifts, the youngsters were given free rein. Among the designers enlisted was Kazuyo Sejima. A prescient choice, Sejima, along with her professional partner Ryue Nishizawa, went on to receive the Pritzker Prize in 2010.

Fronting a suburban train station, Sejima's skinny two-storey building was distinguished by its diminutive stature and bold geometry – a sharp contrast with the surrounding retail sprawl. 'It was a landmark from the plaza as well as the platform', explained Sejima. This effect was achieved with a pair of polished concrete walls that sandwiched the glass roof and a side wall. Everything was pinned together with three cylinders: a circular void cutting through the building, a concealed, round room for resting, and a spiral stair linking the two floors. Jutting outward towards the street, the trapezoidal, glass-encased reception area warmly welcomed visitors.

1994
2008

Architect: Kazuyo Sejima
Location: Tokyo

スクエアビル
パールライスは
おいしいお米の
"しるし"です。

DEEP DIVE

Earthquakes!

In Japan, earthquakes are a way of life. Dedicated evacuation sites dot cities and towns. Duck-and-cover drills occur at schools. And every home has a portable disaster readiness kit equipped with canned food, hard hats and other essentials. The frequent tremors and shakes are never surprising, but they are always unnerving – could this be the Big One?

In fact, many Big Ones have already taken place. The Great Kanto Earthquake in 1923, the Great Hanshin Earthquake in 1995 and the Great East Japan Earthquake in 2011 (followed by a tsunami and a nuclear disaster) all qualify. According to the Tokyo Metropolitan Government, roughly 10 percent of the world's earthquakes occur in Japan – significantly more than anywhere else. One explanation is that the country sits on top of four major tectonic plates. When shifts occur, they propagate shockwaves of various intensities, depending on the location, depth, direction of the movement and other factors. Since the late 19th century, seismic behaviour has fascinated scientists in Japan.

It was the Nobi Earthquake of 1891 that inspired the Tokyo Imperial University professor Toshikata Sano's pioneering investigation into how reinforced concrete construction could promote earthquake resistance.[15] Following in his footsteps, Sano protégés Yoshizo Uchida and Toshiro Kasahara authored Japan's first building and zoning code intended to reduce damage from fires and earthquakes.[16] The ideas put forth by Sano and his disciples were subsequently incorporated into the Building Standards Act of 1950, governing the safety of new construction, including seismic protection.

Over the years this law has been updated repeatedly, including after earthquakes when structural requirements were typically made more stringent and the goal of seismic safety refined. But the basic strategy behind conventional anti-earthquake design remains two-fold: rigidity to withstand seismic forces, and flexibility to dissipate them. While thickening walls, columns and beams can help buildings

(*top*) Great Kanto Earthquake, Tokyo, 1923. (*bottom*) Great Hanshin Earthquake, Kobe, 1995.

stand strong against the shaking, buried rubber padding, springs, ball bearings and the like enable buildings to move with the wobbly ground thereby reducing its impact. Additionally, dampening devices inside act like shock-absorbers to help control vibrations upstairs. Though Japan has been at the forefront of developing these technologies, completely earthquake-proof buildings remain elusive – there are simply too many seismic variables at play. Instead, the goal is to control the degree of damage wrought.

One way this is mitigated is through building inspections during construction, after earthquakes and, periodically, in between. These checks assess structural viability and, hopefully, reduce the possibility of damage or even collapse. If a building does not pass muster, retrofitting for increased strength is a frequent recommendation. For aging buildings constructed in accordance with earlier code requirements, additional steel framing to support concrete or bracing for wood are common requests. But remedies such as these can be expensive and even alter functionality. And so, rightly or wrongly, earthquake safety is often invoked to justify demolition.

Assemble

04

Congregate
Gather
Collect
Convene
Unite
Rally

Tokyu Kaikan + Tokyu Bunka Kaikan

Tokyu Kaikan
1954–2023

Tokyu Bunka
Kaikan
1956–2003

Mixed-used projects of the highest order, these two combined retail and restaurants plus places of assembly and public transportation under one roof. Initially, they helped order the chaos of Tokyo's Shibuya district during its post-World War II reconstruction. But as the area became one of the city's most frenetic commercial centres, these rational buildings had a calming effect. Their stalwart appearances were stabilizing fixtures amid the garish neon, rushing crowds and eateries that change quicker than *kaiten* 'conveyor-belt' sushi.

At the time when this pair arose, however, small stores and tile-roofed homes proliferated in Shibuya, with roads and rail lines crisscrossing hither and thither. Against this backdrop, concrete high-rises must have been quite a sight. This pioneering architecture symbolized Japan's regrowth and heralded its future development. No doubt Junzo Sakakura honed his design sensibility, not to mention his knack for merging architectural and urban design, during a six-year stint in the Paris atelier of Le Corbusier, who championed concrete as well as visionary large-scale developments.

Created in close succession, the two projects were commissioned by the business conglomerate Tokyu Corporation, which developed many transit lines and their surrounding real estate. Integrated with Shibuya Station,

Architect: Junzo Sakakura
Location: Tokyo

Tokyu Kaikan.

Tokyu Kaikan incorporated a subway platform as well as trainline ticket wickets. Floors above and below held the Tokyu Department Store with a theatre above. At street level, the building opened directly onto the plaza where the beloved statue of Hachiko the dog still waits patiently for his owner.

Similarly, an elevated walkway connected Tokyu Bunka Kaikan to the station while separating pedestrians from the onslaught of cars and buses underneath. Truly a place for one-stop shopping, the building held stores, cafés, a rooftop planetarium with its distinctive, silver-coloured dome and a majestic theatre whose stage featured an enormous tapestry curtain designed by none other than Sakakura's mentor, Le Corbusier.

(top) Tokyu Bunka Kaikan.
(opposite) Tokyu Bunka Kaikan theatre with Le Corbusier-designed curtain.

Osaka New Kabuki Theatre

The scene of Japanese dramas festooned with brilliant costumes, mile-high hairdos and acrobatic feats, the Osaka New Kabuki Theatre looked the part. Draped with continuous rows of *karahafu* gables plus a large, tile-clad pitched roof, it oozed tradition despite its mid-century completion. Unsurprisingly, this building was produced by one of Japan's most ambidextrous designers: Togo Murano. He brought about brawny, modern structures made of steel and glass as deftly as delicate works crafted from wood, bamboo and paper. This building stood somewhere in between.

Facing a major boulevard in the centre of the city, this five-storey building had a welcoming colonnaded base where kimono-clad Kabuki enthusiasts could savour a pot of tea or buy a bento lunchbox for sustenance during the lengthy performances – remarkably, eating inside Kabuki theatres remains a time-honoured tradition. Above that was the two-thousand-seat auditorium followed by offices on top. Arranged in a C-shape, the audience was oriented towards the proscenium-style stage but divided by the *hanamachi* runway where actors made running entrances and exits.

1959
2009

Architect: Togo Murano
Location: Osaka

Sogetsu Kaikan

This was the headquarters of the Sogetsu school of *ikebana* flowering arranging but it doubled as a place where creatives of all sorts could exchange ideas. 'It was like an artists' salon', explains architectural historian Saikaku Toyokawa. And that started with the ongoing conversation between the head of the school, Sofu Teshigahara, and his architect friend, Kenzo Tange. Their dialogue was a natural for Tange, who collaborated with Isamu Noguchi, Taro Okamoto, Genichiro Inokuma and other artists from early on in his career.

From its plum Aoyama Street location, Sogetsu's building may have seemed petite, but it had a bold presence. Most of the façade was blanketed with blue ceramic tile outlined in white, and mammoth concrete piers, one per corner, elevated the bulk of the building. These structural gymnastics yielded a see-through slot of space with the main entrance in front and access to the sculpture garden in back. Extending out from the building, its pavers concealed the underground theatre for screening avant-garde films. Upstairs, the building held teaching, administrative and exhibition areas plus a salon where Tange-designed lounge chairs conversed with low tables created by the French architect Charlotte Perriand.

1958
1970s

Architect: Kenzo Tange
Location: Tokyo

La Maison Franco-Japonaise

A collage of forms and finishes, this building was a medium for cultural exchange. Incorporating a theatre, library, meeting rooms and three outdoor plazas, this was a place where the Japanese public could get a taste of France without leaving Tokyo. Appropriately, its designer was Takamasa Yosizaka, who possessed firsthand knowledge of both countries. Though he went on to open his studio in Tokyo, Yosizaka spent some of his early years in the Paris atelier of Le Corbusier where he absorbed his mentor's approach to shape and material.

The building's bold use of concrete echoed Le Corbusier, but its construction was of Japan where designs are refined, and details are worked out in the field. It took full-size models and drawings created in the site office to get the camphorwood handrails just right. 'Yosizaka wondered how it would feel to slide one's hand over the handrail when coming down the stairs or to grab it when going up', recalled former staff member Yuko Saito. The experience of a Yosizaka-designed building was as much about what visitors touched as what they saw.

1959
1995

Architect: Takamasa Yosizaka + Atelier U
Location: Tokyo

日仏会館ホール

Gakushuin University Auditorium

Gakushuin has long been the school of choice for Japan's imperial family and ruling class. Kunio Maekawa was neither a scion of the emperor nor an OB 'Old Boy' alum, but he did bring a fresh take on the school's tree-studded campus. After studying its academic quad, Maekawa proposed adding two rectangular classroom blocks, one square administration building and, in the middle, a pyramid containing a seven-hundred-seat auditorium. Aptly, his wish was to mark the centre of learning with a place for gathering.

'It wasn't a perfect pyramid', explains Isao Hashimoto, representative director of Maekawa Associates. But it was a bold form that stood out from its staid setting. Reflecting the seating and stage inside, the angles of the pyramid's faces were not uniform. Another disparity was the narrow moat outlining the building on three sides, with the entrance on the fourth. To further soften the auditorium's monolithic shape, Maekawa perforated its base with column-like openings and punctured its top. Just below the pyramid's apex he placed a skylight that, together with the circular chandelier, cast gentle light down on the rows of desks below.

1960
2008

Architect: Kunio Maekawa
Location: Tokyo

Imperial Theatre Building

Facing the Imperial Palace and its moat, this was an edifice of importance. It was on this site that Western theatre made its Japanese debut. It was where blockbuster musicals were enjoyed by audiences young and old. And it was here that memories for so many were made.

Together with its neo-classical neighbours, including the insurance company where General Douglas MacArthur was headquartered during the US occupation, the theatre exterior acted the part of unified street wall but inside, over-the-top, dramatic flair took off. A prelude to the performance space, the lobby was dressed to the nines with lavish materials and a show-stopping line-up of architectural artworks. The brilliant colours of artist Genichiro Inokuma's six mural-sized stained-glass windows were enough to make anyone get up and dance. Chandeliers, also by Inokuma, drew the eye upward while stairs at either end led to the theatre entrances upstairs.

Inside, the 1,900-seat auditorium was costumed with an angled ceiling and folded wall panels for acoustics, plus hushed purple seating and green carpeting that did not upstage the show. Hoisted by hydraulic lifts for quick set changes, six revolving stages kept the action rolling.

1966
2025

Architect: Yoshiro Taniguchi
Location: Tokyo

帝国劇場

Aoyama Tower Hall

This double-barrelled project consisted of a high-rise office building plus a low-rise concert hall. Though the two pieces shared a stair and lift core, they were quite independent. No doubt this made it easier to keep the tower up and take the concert hall down. The entire complex faced busy Aoyama Street where generous pavements – a rarity in Tokyo – buffer pedestrians from the rushing cars. The auditorium was set back further by a fountain followed by a paved plaza a few steps up. This public amenity was a place for passersby to take a breather and have a smoke (well, it was the late 1960s). And for concertgoers to prepare for the performance.

The auditorium's entrance was marked by a floating, folded-metal canopy with the building name emblazoned above. Inside, stairs ascended from the foyer to the 220-seat hall where the acoustics were good enough for recordings, thanks to the segmented ceiling and walls. Here it was possible to savour the delicate sound of the piano or violin amid the city's hustle and bustle.

1969
–UNK

Architect: Junzo Yoshimura
Location: Tokyo

AOYAMA TOWER HALL

6

AOYAMA TOWER HALL

Ginza Theatre Building

Clearly Kiyonori Kikutake had a thing for floating buildings. Sky House, his family home, perched on four monolithic piers. His Edo-Tokyo Museum hovered over a public plaza. And his Ginza Theatre Building marked the entrance to its glassed-in ground floor with a pair of super-sized fluted columns that, at least figuratively, did the heavy lifting: overhead, a large solid wall ran straight up to the roof. Fronting the building with a blank façade was a bold move that concealed the 772-seat theatre while tacitly presenting it to the street.

Since 1946, movies have been screened on this site. That was the year when the property's original owner began providing entertainment to Tokyoites reeling from the devastation of World War II. As Japan recovered, Ginza real estate values soared, the theatre changed hands and sequential reconstructions leading up to Kikutake's building occurred.

Facing Ginza's fashionable main boulevard, the skinny twelve-storey building was squeezed between a narrow street and the elevated expressway. It held two theatres (for live performances as well as film), one seventy-seven-room luxury hotel and assorted restaurants. Concentrated on the building's upper floors, the guest accommodations were situated far above the fracas of rushing cars below.

1987
2014

Architect: Kiyonori Kikutake
Location: Tokyo

INFORMATION

Stay

05

Sleep
Lodge
Reside
Dwell
Linger
Rest

Harumi Apartments

'The Harumi Apartments were both Kunio Maekawa's first and last high-rise apartment building', remarks Isao Hashimoto, representative director, Maekawa Associates. It was also the first tall building undertaken by the Japan Housing Corporation or JHC (now the Urban Renaissance Agency), a government-sponsored organization launched in the early 1950s. At that time Japan faced an acute housing shortage due to the devastation of World War II. The JHC responded by constructing low-scale subsidized housing and granting loans to homeowners wishing to rebuild. As the economy improved and people began migrating to urban areas in search of better employment, the agency turned to large residential developments in and around major cities. For this ten-storey apartment building planned for reclaimed land in Tokyo Bay, they hired Kunio Maekawa.

The Harumi Apartments' defining feature was its hefty structural system, a reflection of what Hashimoto terms Maekawa's 'technical approach' to architecture. More than aesthetic preference or stylistic trend, Maekawa sought the honest expression of materials and technology. Here, this took the form of a colossal reinforced concrete frame that met the ground with flared, buttress-like column bases. Within this matrix a secondary grid divided each opening into six apartments.

1958
1996

Architect: Kunio Maekawa
Location: Tokyo

15

The bold appearance of Maekawa's building has been likened to the high-rise concrete apartment building in Marseilles, the Unité d'Habitation created by Le Corbusier, the Paris-based architect for whom Maekawa worked in the 1930s.[17] According to Hashimoto, another similarity was the 'skip floor strategy' of locating the communal corridors only on every third floor (with small stairs leading to the apartments on the levels in between). This layout reduced the overall amount of circulation space. It also enabled fresh air and daylight to enter the apartment at both ends on the intervening floors where the units extended the full building width since there were no public hallways. Covered exterior spaces, these corridors doubled as social places where children played while their parents chatted – much like neighbours on narrow residential streets anywhere in Japan.

Maekawa recognized the value of integrating East and West for the private quarters too. Within each apartment he placed tatami-mat and wood-floored rooms side by side and linked them with sliding paper screens. Thanks to foldable futon mattresses, the former served as both the living and bedroom room while the latter held the foyer, eat-in kitchen, toilet and, appropriately, a Japanese-style bath.

Hotel Okura

When it comes to understated elegance, the Hotel Okura was in a class of its own. Its sublime lobby designed by Yoshiro Taniguchi epitomized Japanese Modernism. Segueing smoothly from the reception area, it was the place to see and be seen. Among the room's most striking features were its generously spaced seating areas. Resembling plum blossoms, each one centred on a lacquered table surrounded by upholstered chairs with splayed, petal-shaped backs. Suspended from the double-height ceiling, long hexagonal pendant lights and boxy floor fixtures reminiscent of traditional *andon* lamps filled the room with soft, ambient light. While a mural-sized map highlighting world time zones elicited fantasies of faraway lands, *shoji*-clad window walls directed the eye towards the garden just outside.

Located on a former aristocratic estate, the hotel sat back from the street, enabling an appreciation of Hideo Kosaka's patterned exterior and deep roof eaves, as well as ceremonious arrivals from the street. At the entrance, eager bellhops readily welcomed guests. Realized during Japan's meteoric economic growth, the Okura was where business deals were hatched, movies were filmed and a steady stream of US presidents caught much needed shuteye.

1962
2015

Architects: Yoshio Taniguchi with
Hideo Kosaka and others
Location: Tokyo

Hotel Fujita

Embodying *omotenashi*, Japan's unique hospitality, the Hotel Fujita was a fan favourite. Everyone from local citizens to international celebrities stayed here – and with good reason. It was conveniently located in the heart of Kyoto, the country's capital of traditional culture and history. It offered eating and entertainment options for various appetites. And it occupied a splendid state-of-the-art building designed by Junzo Yoshimura.

Running alongside the Kamo River, the seven-storey hotel paralleled the water with its long, low shape. This geometry was underscored by the horizontal lines of the protective eaves above the guestroom windows, which opened to river views and the city's twinkling lights beyond. The presence of water also characterized the lower floors where dining and lounge areas were oriented towards a sunken pond integrated with the building. Like Kyoto's famous gardens, the manmade pool with its artfully placed plantings, rock assemblages and rushing waterfalls evoked the natural world. *Fluid*, the mural created for the lounge by artist and close friend of Yoshimura, Genichiro Inokuma, offered yet another water reference. Fortunately, this exquisite work was salvaged by the Marugame Genichiro-Inokuma Museum of Contemporary Art when the building came down.

1970
2011

Architect: Junzo Yoshimura
Location: Kyoto

Nakagin Capsule Tower

Facing a busy thoroughfare at the edge of Tokyo's fashionable Ginza business district, the Nakagin Capsule Tower was a local landmark. It was also one of the best examples of Metabolism ever realized. Japan's only homegrown modern architecture movement, Metabolism debuted at the World Design Conference held in 1960 in Tokyo. Though its proponents approached the concept in various ways, they shared the view that cities and buildings could be conceived as organic frameworks. Even if made of concrete and steel, their components could be modified or even swapped out in the future. This logic paved the way for partial renewal instead of full-scale redevelopment. But it also derived from Japan's age-old practice of replacing parts piecemeal, be it a torn *shoji* paper screen or a gnarled roof beam. Kisho Kurokawa intended his Nakagin Capsule Tower to be a Metabolist case in point.

The backbones of Kurokawa's structure were a pair of concrete and steel frame towers, eleven and thirteen stories respectively, joined by bridges at three levels. Cantilevered from the towers with four tension bolts apiece were 140 capsules, each one an efficiency apartment. Measuring just two-and-a-half by three-and-a-half metres (eight by twelve feet), every boxlike unit was scaled like a traditional Japanese tearoom (which comes as no surprise since Kurokawa was a tea ceremony aficionado) but fashioned like a futuristic spaceship capsule. One wall contained

1970
2022

Architect: Kisho Kurokawa
Location: Tokyo

中銀
中銀
Ginza
DAI-ICHI
HOTEL

an assortment of built-in features, including storage, an air conditioner for heating as well as cooling, a colour television and a foldout desk. There was also a two-burner cooktop and a mini fridge in addition to an array of optional items, such as stereo, tape deck and desk calculator.

Opposite this loaded wall stood a 'unit bath' made of moulded plastic that integrated the toilet, sink and a deep Japanese-style tub. Saving precious inches, it was accessed through an angled door with nautical rounded corners and portholes for light and ventilation. This left just enough room to tuck in a double bed beneath the circular window at the end of each box. Dotted with these round openings and oriented in different directions, the stacked boxes gave the building its distinctive appearance.

Each capsule was made of lightweight steel at a shipping-container fabricator and then installed on site. The ease of construction and compact space appealed to Kurokawa so much that he subsequently used capsules for his weekend home, Capsule House K.

SONY
SONY

Sky Building No. 5

Youji Watanabe's Sky Building No. 5 was affectionately known as the Godzilla Building. Indeed, its steeply angled profile coupled with a prow-like protuberance (containing a machine room) bore a resemblance to the fictional monster of Japanese film who debuted in 1954. But this unique geometry also attested to the architect's deep-seated love of the sea and sea-faring vessels – a theme that washed up in many of his buildings.

Unsurprisingly, Watanabe, the scion of a long line of carpenters, grew up in a Niigata Prefecture fishing port on the Japan Sea coast. As a boy, he frequently demonstrated his prowess for model ship-making, but it wasn't until many years later that the motif began to surface in his architectural work. '[T]he image of the ship ... represents [Watanabe's] longing for the pure, free world promised by the sea', explained Professor Takashi Hasegawa.[18]

Anchored firmly to the ground, the base of the eleven-storey structure contained small shops with balconied apartments filling the floors above. From each unit an angled exhaust air pipe extended upward. 'They looked like the bones of a bird wing', commented architect Takeshi Sato, Watanabe's nephew. Conspicuously absent was the roof. Instead, the pointy building top enabled sunlight to reach street level.

1971 –UNK

Architect: Youji Watanabe
Location: Tokyo

Hotel Beverly Tom

A sturdy cylinder capped with a lacy steel dome, the Hotel Beverly Tom looked more like a 'love hotel' than a wedding venue. While this bold form may have been less conspicuous amid the brawn of Tomakomai City, an industrial port where big boats prepare for Pacific voyages, a non-denominational chapel for church nuptials (religion not included) stood next door. Unsurprisingly, Hokkaido – Japan's northernmost island – is better known for agriculture than architecture, even more so in the 1970s. But for some designers it was an open playing field. Having grown up here, Minoru Takeyama, who had studios in Tokyo as well as Sapporo, built several experimental works around the island.

This hotel took the form of a mini tower with a C-shaped plan encircling a hollow core open to the see-through dome and the starry sky beyond. Entered diagonally from the street, visitors proceeded into the lobby, with the restaurant in back and tube-shaped lifts in the middle. These led to the guest rooms upstairs followed by the roof terrace and observation deck. Dotted with its own twinkling lights, the ethereal orb drew the eye upward, leaving the city behind.

1973 –UNK

Architect: Minoru Takeyama
Location: Hokkaido

Akasaka Prince Hotel

A V-shaped tower dressed in reflective aluminium, the Akasaka Prince Hotel was hard to miss, whether you were scooting past on the Shuto Expressway or strolling leisurely around the Imperial Palace moat. This striking form with its saw-toothed profile and shiny surface could grab anyone's attention. Unsurprisingly, it was constructed at a time when Japanese hotel buildings were still heroic, and their range of services far exceeded the provision of places to bed down.

Preceded by a grand plaza, the hotel entrance was positioned at the convergence of the tower's two halves – the building's angled shape tacitly pointed the way in. Some visitors came for the restaurants, shops, exhibition hall and, of course, the five-hundred-seat ballroom – a veritable hall of mirrors – concentrated in the low-scale block in front. Others ascended to one of the one thousand guestrooms occupying most of the forty-storey wings. Oriented at forty-five-degree angles in relation to the corridor, the rooms had distinct sleeping and seating areas plus drop-dead gorgeous Tokyo views. Everyone brushed shoulders in the main lobby, which was open to a sunken courtyard ringed by shops and restaurants. 'The sight of people coming and going must be a very interesting scene to the people in the Coffee Terrace below', mused Tange.[19]

1982
2013

Architect: Kenzo Tange
Location: Tokyo

Bizan Hall

Designed for Shizuoka Seika High School, Bizan Hall sat amid a residential neighbourhood hemmed in by houses; the only street connection was a narrow strip of land that held its portico. In deference to the neighbours, architect Itsuko Hasegawa limited herself to two stories but blanketed most of the land with a building composed of a wedge-shaped entry pavilion plus a square block surrounding a central courtyard. Dividing the building in two reduced its bulk but also hinted at its complex interior that served graduates, teachers, students and staff. 'I have long believed that a building used by numerous people should not be a single volume but rather a multiplicity, like a city', wrote Hasegawa.[20]

Inside, Hasegawa provided rooms of three sizes – small, medium and large – without assigning functions. While the biggest hall could accommodate dining and lectures downstairs, cell-like cubicles upstairs held folding beds for overnight visitors. To control noise from propagating outward, Hasegawa minimized perimeter windows, oriented the rooms inward and topped many with operable skylights for daylight and fresh air. From above, the collection of cupolas looked like an urban roofscape in miniature.

1984
1989

Architect: Itsuko Hasegawa
Location: Shizuoka Prefecture

清水銀行

Roppongi Prince Hotel

The short-lived Roppongi Prince Hotel was a product of Japan's bubble economy when mind-boggling architecture kept popping up all over. It was a time when consumers, not to mention architectural clients, had money to burn. Located at the edge of Roppongi, a teaming nightlife district, this building mitigated its awkward hillside site and met the street with a boxy exterior enclosed with elegant white walls. But bright Kabuki-red columns ushered guests into the ground-floor lobby with its tropical fish tank – a portent of what was to come.

Inside, wavy walls wrapped a central courtyard with an open-air swimming pool in the middle. While guest rooms occupied the upper floors, assorted bars and restaurants encircled the courtyard below. Filled with sparkling blue water year-round, the pool's curvaceous form was outlined with clear acrylic. The sight of frolicking bathers provided constant entertainment for those nursing gin & tonics nearby. It was 'chic and fun', in the words of architect Kisho Kurokawa.

1984
2012

Architect: Kisho Kurokawa
Location: Tokyo

Carlsberg

Hotel Sofitel Tokyo

Tiered like a pagoda, the Hotel Sofitel Tokyo (née Cosima) didn't just stand at the edge of Ueno district's idyllic Shinobazu Pond populated with lotus flowers and swan boats. It also towered over the neighbourhood's in-your-face eat-and-drink buildings, brimming with tiny bars and restaurants, budget big box stores and, of course, love hotels to beat the band. Unlike these eye-catching but weirdly windowless buildings intended for private dalliances, Kikutake's high-rise hotel offered spectacular views as well as easy access to Ueno's array of museums, temples and shrines.

What greeted the clientele upon their arrival was a very tall building with a very small footprint. Jutting out on either side were stepped blocks of guest rooms cantilevered off a central core containing lifts and glassed-in staircases. Even for Tokyo, this really was a stand-out structure.

As in many hotels, periodic room refreshening was a given due to wear and tear. And a good fit with Kikutake's Metabolist approach, which promoted architecture with changeable parts. 'In a lot of his buildings the exterior was fixed but the interior could be changed', explained Professor Shingo Saito. But the hotel underwent more than an upgrade when the entire building was taken down after a mere fourteen years.

1994
2008

Architect: Kiyonori Kikutake
Location: Tokyo

SOFITEL
SOFITEL

Yusuhara Visitors' Centre

When it comes to the Japanese practice of *shinrin-yoku* or forest-bathing, few places can compare to Yusuhara. Trees abound in this mountainous Shikoku Island community. Since the 1980s, Kengo Kuma has completed several works here, including the town office, public library and a gallery resembling a traditional wooden bridge. Each one was moulded by the area's culture and climate but especially the Visitors' Centre, where travellers tasted home-grown foods, appreciated local woodworking skills and soaked up the scenery.

This municipal facility consisted of three components aligned in a row: restaurant, lodging and communal bath. Hovering lightly above, the long roof was a riff on Yusuhara's nickname: 'the town above the clouds'. Meanwhile, a circular pool extended out from the bottom of the building. On its far side, a square stage for traditional music and dance performances floated on the glassy surface while the water flowed gently over the pool's edge, as if linking the manmade and natural. Barely separated by a glass window wall, both restaurant patrons and overnight guests could enjoy the water and the lush landscape beyond.

1994
2022

Architect: Kengo Kuma
Location: Kochi Prefecture

The Curious Case of the Imperial – The Hotel that Keeps Reinventing Itself

In Europe and North America, historic hotels are nostalgically celebrated. In Japan, however, few reach that status. When their buildings wear out, they come down and that's the end of it. Bucking this trend, Tokyo's Imperial Hotel is an epic and exceptional tale of architectural renewal and institutional rebirth. It spans the construction of four buildings: Yuzuru Watanabe's Second Empire-style edifice completed in 1890, Frank Lloyd Wright's 'Crown Jewel of the Orient' in 1923, Teitaro Takahashi's streamlined tower in 1970, and now Tsuyoshi Tane's structure, scheduled to open in 2036. In terms of size, function and architectural expression, each one differs decisively from its predecessor, yet they have more in common than meets the eye. All have occupied the same property near the Imperial Palace. And all proudly acknowledge the hotel's past while embracing societal change – the guiding principle promulgated by the Imperial's first chairman, Eiichi Shibusawa.

Under the aegis of Shibusawa and other business leaders, the first Imperial Hotel arose shortly after Japan ended some two hundred years of near isolation and opened its doors to other countries at the start of the Meiji era (1868–1912). Though traditional *ryokan* inns abounded, there was need for a Western-style guesthouse for foreign dignitaries. Appropriately, the commission went to Yuzuru Watanabe, a former student of Josiah Conder, the imported British architect and founder of Japan's first school of architecture. A three-storey wood frame structure with a mansard roof, Watanabe's stately building contained sixty guest rooms. But in a matter of years the hotel was too small for the growing numbers of overseas visitors and a decision was made to replace it with a much bigger building designed by the American architect Frank Lloyd Wright.

Wright's H-shaped building was essentially symmetrical in plan and interspersed with void spaces – a large

(*top*) The Imperial Hotel, Yuzuru Watanabe, 1890.
(*bottom*) The Imperial Hotel, Frank Lloyd Wright, 1923.

IMPERIAL HOTEL

pool in front and courtyard gardens beyond. Set back from the street, it stepped up gradually, reaching three stories towards the rear of the site. In addition to 270 guest rooms, Wright's hotel incorporated a wide array of other functions, such as a theatre, ballroom, restaurant and shopping arcade, as well as vendors for wedding celebrations. The Imperial was no longer just a place to stay. Amazingly, its opening day coincided with the Great Kanto Earthquake. Yet Wright's building stood strong, a miracle that architectural historian Ken Tadashi Oshima attributes to floating foundations inspired by Chicago's early skyscrapers.[21] While Wright took his usual soup-to-nuts stance by designing everything from the exterior tiles to the dining room teacups, he prioritized local materials such as Oya stone quarried in Tochigi Prefecture, and bricks made in Aichi Prefecture.

By the 1960s, however, Wright's hotel had become weary and worn. It seemed old, out of date and incompatible with Japan's growing prosperity and popularity. Despite vigorous protests around the globe, demolition befell Wright's masterpiece in 1968, but with the directive to resurrect the hotel's main entrance pavilion at the open-air architecture museum, Meiji Mura.

The plan to rebuild was also a response to Japan's continuing uptick in tourism. The hosting of the 1964 Tokyo Olympics, the upcoming 1970 Osaka Expo and the arrival of the jumbo jet rendered Japan a sought-after travel destination. This time the redesign was entrusted to Teitaro Takahashi, an established architect with hotel experience. Takahashi's soaring verticality was a striking contrast to Wright's sweeping horizontality. It featured a seventeen-storey tower fronted by a low building that bowed politely to Hibiya Park across the street and the Imperial Palace nearby. The hotel was entered through a porte cochère where chauffeured cars and colourful taxis awaited passengers. From here, the expansive lobby led to more than seven hundred guestrooms, plus shopping, dining and other amenities, including the Old Imperial Bar, a relic of Wright's legacy, and Togo Murano's Toko-An traditional tea ceremony room. But after fifty years, the hotel's management once again faced the conundrum of whether to renovate.

After agreeing to replace the building, a competition was held in 2021 to select the architect. This time it had to be someone who had never designed a hotel, was internationally active (but not an overly busy starchitect) and was under sixty due to the project's long lead time. The choice of Paris-based Tsuyoshi Tane not only satisfied these criteria, it granted this important commission to an architect who prioritizes history. 'When I start to work on a project, archaeology is my point of view', explains Tane. Just how this translates to his update of the Imperial remains to be seen. But one thing is for sure: Tane will have plenty of material to work with.

(*opposite, top*) The Imperial Hotel, Teitaro Takahashi, 1970.
(*opposite, bottom*) The Imperial Hotel lobby interior, Teitaro Takahashi, 1970.

Work

06

Labour
Toil
Grind
Produce
Engineer

Janome Sewing Machine Building

A leading producer of sewing machines dating back to the 1920s, the Janome Corporation is known for needle-art innovations. This included the round metal bobbin thought to resemble a *janome*, or snake's eye, after which the company was named. Another breakthrough was hiring Kunio Maekawa to design their new Tokyo headquarters. Motivated by technical knowhow, Maekawa utilized prefabricated pieces – walls, floors, structure and others – that stitched together as easily as bolts of cloth.

The most visible of these elements were the cross-shaped, pre-cast concrete units forming the main façade. This tartan grid of metal, masonry and glass rested on the building's colonnaded base. Open to the street as well as fronting the building, this conduit knitted architecture and urban fabric together – a frequent theme in Maekawa's work. 'It was like a traditional *kairo* covered cloister [in Buddhist temples]', recalled Maekawa Associates' representative director, Isao Hashimoto. Walking through this outdoor passage, pedestrians could peer through the window wall at the array of Janome's latest offerings. Each machine was highlighted on a pedestal in the ground-floor showroom, a double-height space with a mezzanine connected by a spiral stair. Stacked above that were office floors tailored to fit within the area's then legal height limit.

1965 –UNK

Architect: Kunio Maekawa
Location: Tokyo

OME
JANOME
JANOME

Nomura Display Co., Ltd.

Osaka Branch
1965–UNK

Tokyo Branch
1966, 1974–UNK

During his stint in Japan's navy, Kiyoshi Seike designed many aircraft hangars. But factories? They were uncharted territory – that is until he landed a pair of commissions from the exhibition and event planners, Nomura Display Co., Ltd. First came their Osaka headquarters; Tokyo followed soon after. Each job consisted of offices plus a factory (with a second Tokyo office building added later). Looking the part of a business in the promotion business, Seike's buildings were crisp, elegant and, starting with their façades, made positive first impressions on potential clients.

Concerning building fronts, Seike had this to say: '[a] Western façade is a wall, but a Japanese façade is not much more than doors and *shoji* screens'.[22] The Nomura buildings were mash-ups of both. Upstairs, the Osaka offices were encased with tubes of translucent glass – an industrial product that admitted soft daylight, much like rice paper. Downstairs, the reception area and adjacent factory presented with gridded glass block reminiscent of the traditional screens and their wood mullions. This geometry was expanded at the second Tokyo office building, which was covered with a large grid of glass and steel. Downstairs, see-through window walls completely opened the building base to the street in front and a canal in back.

Architect: Kiyoshi Seike
Locations: Osaka / Tokyo

(*top*) Toyko branch.
(*bottom*) Osaka branch.

Dentsu Tsukiji Building

At the outset, this building was envisioned not just as the headquarters for Japan's largest ad agency. It also was conceived as a catalysing urban device that could be cloned repeatedly to promote the redevelopment of Tsukiji, a central Tokyo neighbourhood famous for its now defunct fish market. But when Dentsu's president died suddenly, this ambitious concept was scrapped, and Kenzo Tange's design was scaled down to a single building.

For his first scheme, the architect proposed Corten steel façades (which might have dripped rusty water on passersby during the rainy season). But the completed building was made of exposed concrete that gave it a commanding presence among the nondescript offices and shops nearby. Standing out from the pack, its exterior was defined by a matrix of beams and columns that tapered as they ascended towards the roof – a visually subtle but nonetheless dynamic touch. In between, they framed deep-set octagonal window openings that enlivened the office floors with daylight and distant views.

1967
2021

Architect: Kenzo Tange
Location: Tokyo

Industrial Bank of Japan

The headquarters of what was then one of Japan's most powerful banks, Togo Murano's heroic building totally looked the part. This was the place where titans of industry sought financing to develop the country's shipbuilding, steel manufacturing and other big businesses. This was the place where Japan's best and brightest made the decisions that fuelled the so-called post-war 'economic miracle'. And this was the place that exemplified Murano's architectural might. Unmoved by stylistic trends or schools of thought, this highly prolific architect realized some three hundred projects – among them some of the most expressive works built in Japan.

For the bank, this took the form of a fifteen-storey wedge-shaped edifice that capitalized on the site's rather awkward oblong shape in the middle of Tokyo's Marunouchi business district. Taking his cues from the property's proportions, Murano concentrated the bank's offices in the site's wider portion. Where the building's long outer walls converged, its width narrowed down to a mere sixteen metres (fifty-two feet) – a unique geometry that gave rise to the moniker 'battleship building'. Yet facing one of the area's main avenues, Eitai Dori, with just a sliver of building, was a bold response by any metric. This skinniness seemed antithetical to an institution of this stature, but this smallness made a big impact.

1974
2017

Architect: Togo Murano
Location: Tokyo

On top of its narrow width, the corner of the building didn't even touch the ground. Instead of anchoring it below, Murano carved out the base and left it hanging – a gravity-defying stunt enabled by a curved cantilever support. In the open space beneath the looming arch, Murano placed a small pool, which was eventually filled in with plantings that obviously had no need for sunlight. Though structural innovation was not Murano's jam, he employed it skilfully in service to his architecture.

Everywhere else, the building's weightiness was practically palpable. Especially outside, where reddish-brown granite from South Dakota encased the entire structure with the impenetrability of, well, a bank vault. Except for the vertical strips of windows fronting the offices from street level to roofline, the smooth stone was devoid of ornament or visible detailing. But its polished surface was enlivened by the reflection of the buildings across the street. Abutting the building base, the stone was given a matte finish and turned into the pavement. Integrated with fabric of the city, Murano's building was very much a monument – without being monumental.

Tokyo Marine and Fire Insurance Building

This Maekawa masterpiece was one of Tokyo's most distinctive tall buildings. Its elegant form – twin rectangles robed with brick-coloured tile – occupied a prominent corner. In one direction it faced the imperial moat and in the other the broad avenue extending from the palace grounds to majestic Tokyo Station. Whether passing on foot or by car, this was a building that caught your eye – and made you want to look again. Set back by an expansive plaza, the edifice looked like the home of a corporate giant. Yet its outward appearance contrasted sharply with the coolness of conventional glass and steel skyscrapers. A curious blend of old and new, its thick façades were richly textured and warmly coloured, as if acknowledging Japan's brick government buildings nearby, which date back to the Meiji era (1868–1912).

Though this was the only skyscraper that Maekawa ever brought to life, the architect had a clear idea of how big buildings ought to engage their surroundings. 'He said build tall but keep the base open for pedestrians', explains Isao Hashimoto, Maekawa Associates' representative director. No doubt this strategy bore the influence of Le Corbusier, the Paris-based architect and urbanist for whom Maekawa worked prior to launching his own studio in Tokyo.

Illustrating this point, Maekawa invited passersby to interact with his building by traversing its plaza and dropping in to visit its sunken garden. The building itself began with

1974
2023

Architect: Kunio Maekawa
Location: Tokyo

a colonnaded base that created a slot of covered exterior space – Japan's traditional way of softening a hard division between inside and out. Maekawa further blurred that boundary by using the exterior pavers for the floor of the column-free lobby. This engineering feat was pulled off by concentrating structural and other vertical elements in a central core (it stood where the two rectangular volumes overlapped) and tasking the hefty exterior walls with the heavy lifting. More than mere window dressing, the gridded façades doubled as the support system. In the words of critic Hiroshi Watanabe, they formed a kind of 'exoskeleton'.[23]

Extending from the ground to the roof, the columns joined forces with horizontal beams to create the building's signature exterior, with deep-set windows filling the voids in between. Like his mentor, Maekawa initially gravitated towards exposed concrete. Yet, after recognizing the material's inherent weakness, he began protecting it with tile that could extend the life of his buildings – a choice befitting an insurance company headquarters.

Komatsu Building

Bold and brawny, the Komatsu Building was in a class of its own. Commensurate with its titanic role in the world of heavy equipment manufacturing – tractors, bulldozers and other hulking vehicles – it had a commanding presence both from the street and from the elevated Shuto Expressway whose inner ring ran right past Komatsu's central Tokyo corner site.

Complying with the city's height restrictions of the mid-1960s, the ten-storey building was covered with Greek marble. This weighty material conveyed strength, solidity and even a whiff of permanence. While a parade of industrial-strength arches with angled profiles marched around the building's base, ribbons of elongated, hexagonal windows wrapped the walls above. This was a façade with rhythm, eye-appeal and a decidedly unique character.

The richness carried over inside where green onyx lined the lobby. Like many office buildings of its vintage, this was primarily a company workspace, but it offered consumer amenities too. While an underground arcade was filled with shops and restaurants, the rooftop garden famous for its flowering cherry trees was open to the public as well. Though the building couldn't be saved from the wrecking ball, the beloved trees were salvaged and hoisted away before demolition.

1966
2024

Architects: Makoto Masuzawa + Katsumi Nakayama
Location: Tokyo

東洋信託銀行

Shuko-sha Building

Seven doors, five going nowhere. It might have seemed odd, even uninviting, to begin a building with a somewhat grand semi-circular entrance with inoperable doors, complete with misleading handles. How many times were visitors duped by Arata Isozaki's ruse? But such was the way into this exuberant little printing and advertising company. Perhaps this gesture offered a glimpse of its many quirks – bridges, bursts of colour and spiral stairs – tidily packaged by the gridded exterior wrapping.

On the outside, the entire five-storey building was awash in squares: sheets of travertine and glass galore. The division of solid and see-through loosely corresponded to the inner workings. The lower two floors held galleries, an exhibition hall and other rooms related to cultural events hosted here. Connected by an internal spiral stair, the workspaces were concentrated on the two upper floors, followed by the company president's suite above. Instead of concealing the lift in a corner, Isozaki placed its shaft squarely in the middle of the frontmost room, enabling people to circulate around it or ride upstairs. At the top, the lift gave access to an open walkway that offered panoramic city views, no doubt a great way for the president to start his day.

1975 –UNK

Architect: Arata Isozaki
Location: Fukuoka Prefecture

Hanae Mori Building

Likened to the Champs-Elysées, tree-lined Omotesando got its start as a fashion street in the 1950s when Japan was in the throes of the Allied occupation, and Western-style clothing was in demand. Being proximate to Washington Heights, where US army families lived, this area was the ideal spot for designers skilled at sewing party dresses and skirt suits. One of the most enterprising was Hanae Mori, who went on to build a fashion empire with a swish headquarters clad entirely in mirrored glass.

One of Omotesando's first fashion flagships, this shiny building brilliantly reflected the zelkova trees lining the boulevard in front. But it also reflected a turning point in Kenzo Tange's career – from concrete public buildings to flashy commissions from wealthy overseas clients. Like an abstract butterfly – Mori's signature motif – her building's nearly symmetrical plan stepped back from the street with a promenade in the middle with wings on either side. At street level they held a bank, shops and the Hanae Mori boutique, while models strutted their stuff and other company business took place upstairs.

1979
2011

Architect: Kenzo Tange
Location: Tokyo

HANAE MORI

Dai-ichi Kangyo Bank Head Office

Spawned by the merging of two major banks, this thirty-two-storey building made a statement in central Tokyo. 'It was designed to last for 100 to 200 years', remarks architect Taro Ashihara, the architect's son. The complex's defining element was an office tower clad with tinted glass and white granite flanked by low-scale halls for lectures and banking. Extending out like an apron, the banking floor greeted customers. Inside, it read as a large, square hall defined by a semi-circular seating area surrounding the Giacomo Manzù sculpture, *Dopo La Danza* (After the Dance). At the time of construction, public art was not the norm in Japan but here it was a priority. Overhead, a tilted glass roof shielded with aluminium louvres admitted soft daylight. Warm and inviting, this was a place that encouraged people to linger.

Another public amenity was the pedestrian mall stretching the length of the building's south side. Running alongside a linear pond, this stepped walkway was enlivened with planters, lighting and artworks. 'My father was influenced by Paley Park in New York', explains Ashihara. Similarly, this space was a welcome respite for everyone amid the city's hustle and bustle.

1981
2024

Architect: Yoshinobu Ashihara
Location: Tokyo

Promote

07

Present
Introduce
Champion
Endorse
Boost
Display

Kobe Newspaper Hall

A commanding presence capped with colossal signage, the Kobe Newspaper Hall was a local landmark until 1995 when the Great Hanshin Earthquake levelled vast portions of the city and its surroundings. Prior to its demise, this huge seven-storey structure stood opposite the Sannomiya Station, a regional transportation hub in the centre of Kobe's business and entertainment district. '[It] acquired a symbolic presence in front of the station', wrote Kazuto Kasahara of Kyoto Institute of Technology.[24] A city within a city, the building contained not just the newspaper's editorial offices but also its printing facility and a variety of commercial ventures open to the public.

Bands of windows and balconies emphasized the building's great span, but its most stand-out feature was the four-storey mini building perched on top. Jutting skyward, this tiny tower visually balanced all that horizontality. Initially it offered views in multiple directions, but these were compromised by later additions on either side. Yet filling out the roof did not impede its other important and very lucrative function: sign display. From the 1950s onward, Japan began capping buildings with some of the world's most eye-popping and most photographed signage – signatures of industry literally supported by architecture. Going above and beyond print media, this building's pedestal-like top broadcast its message for all to see.

1956
1995

Architect: Togo Murano
Location: Hyogo Prefecture

National
Matsushita Electric
金龍閣
山一證券
神戸新聞
デイリースポーツ

San-ai Dream Centre

The equivalent of Manhattan's 57th and 5th, the Ginza 4-Chome intersection is where Tokyo's stylish and elegant convene. One corner holds the home of Seiko watches – the venerated Wako Building, fittingly topped with a clocktower. Another, the majestic Mitsukoshi Department Store where twin lion statues mark the entrance. And, kitty-corner, stood the San-ai Dream Centre: a futuristic mini tower created by Shoji Hayashi, head designer of the architecture and engineering firm, Nikken Sekkei.

Despite the site's prominence, its tiny, 293-square-metre (3,154-square-foot) footprint[25] severely limited its commercial potential. Making the most of the land's location, Hayashi proposed a 'cylinder of light symbolizing the vibrancy of Ginza'.[26] Fortunately, Kiyoshi Ichimura, the property's owner and founder of Ricoh Company, Ltd., followed his architect's advice.

Naturally, Hayashi wanted as much transparency as possible to allow the building to emanate a glow. So, he devised a curved glass and steel exterior skin – a first for Japan, according to architect and Hayashi assistant Koichi Yasuda. In addition, the nine-storey tube-shaped structure culminated in a drum-shaped neon sign. Location, lighting and a diminutive size packed a punch, captivating pedestrians as well as tram passengers (at that time streetcars ran down the centre of Ginza's main avenues) who rode by. What they saw was more than just look-at-me architecture. Here

1962
2023

Architect: Shoji Hayashi / Nikken Sekkei
Location: Tokyo

TRIC MFG CO.
San-ai

was a building that symbolized Japan's rising technological might and robust economy.

Due to low-rise shops on either side, the conventional staging of construction next door was impossible. Instead, this took place on the site itself. First a four-storey base hugging the property lines and central, circular stair-lift core had to be built. After that, the core was used to lift ring-shaped concrete floor slabs into place.

Occupied by the fashion brand San-ai, the showrooms inside were created by the tenant's in-house designer, Shiro Kuramata, who later became one of Japan's most visionary interior and furniture designers. His transparent display cases coupled with ceiling-mounted strip lighting radiating out from the core were the stuff of, well, dreams.

SONY Building

In 1957, the SONY Corporation rocked the world by introducing the first dual-band transistor radio.[27] Less than ten years later, the electronics giant wowed audiences again with the opening of the SONY Building on a busy corner at Ginza's Sukiyabashi Crossing. Contrasting with the area's blaring neon, pedestrian crowds and streams of cars, the two-part building consisted of a rectangular volume wrapped with aluminium louvres plus a white, antenna-like lift tower adorned with a mosaic of moving lights made with 2,300 cathode-ray tube TVs plus 'SONY' emblazoned in large red letters. Here was an architecture that stood out from its site but harmonized perfectly with the sleek precision and functional beauty of SONY's products.

Instead of broadcasting its contents outward like a conventional advertisement tower, the interior was all but concealed. More akin to *shoji* paper panels than standard shop windows, the metal screens revealed little of the building's inner workings. Neither a manufacturing facility nor an administrative centre, its sole purpose was to promote SONY goods to consumers. 'In terms of building type and space, it was very unique,' says Taro Ashihara, the architect's architect son.

Inside, his father created a spiralling sequence of showrooms inspired by the popular pastime known as *Ginbura* or strolling, shopping and eating in Ginza.

1966
2017

Architect: Yoshinobu Ashihara
Location: Tokyo

GINZA
山一證券
フルヤ
FURUYA
大和證券
SONY
SONY

Extending their walks inside, visitors took SONY's lift up and then meandered down on foot while admiring the latest TVs and tape recorders. While the two top floors held a performance hall and a restaurant, the lower six floors were each divided into four platform-like levels that pinwheeled around a central column. Separated by ninety-centimetre (thirty-five-inch) gaps, the mini floors were connected by short runs of stairs, enabling a sense of continuity from top to bottom. At street level, stairs leading to the basement acted like a giant keyboard, emitting a do, re or mi with each step.

Another unusual feature was the outdoor plaza in front of the building – a rare public amenity in Japan at that time. Yoshinobu Ashihara explained: 'I wanted to create a miniature square, which though small – like a SONY transistor perhaps – would offer the people of Tokyo something similar to what Rockefeller Centre offers New Yorkers'.[28] A sunken garden at times, a place for installations at others, this open space was a gift to the city.

Toho Twin Tower Building

For the sophisticated entertainment seeker, old-school art connoisseur or discerning shopper, there is no place like Ginza. Unsurprisingly, it was in this milieu that the Toho Twin Tower Building stood. Belonging to one of Japan's premier film production companies, it was an elegant structure wrapped entirely in white aluminium perforated with lozenge-shaped windows and pleated like an accordion – a move that enabled the building to effortlessly round the site's corners. While commercial tenants on the ground floor benefitted from steady pedestrian traffic, the twin towers above – the building's namesake – reached for the stars.

Like many prominent buildings in Ginza and other commercial hubs – think Shinjuku and Shibuya – the top of the Toho Twin Tower Building proved to be the perfect stage for signage. From the get-go it was an advertising opportunity waiting to happen. And when that did occur, the roof's dramatis personae – the twin towers – were bound together by a broad sign-band promoting the Fuji Electric Co., Ltd. This merging of architecture and advertising capitalized on the building's visibility, no doubt brought in big bucks and, appropriately, had a starring role in Ginza's megawatt neon narrative.

1969
2020

Architects: Yoshiro Taniguchi (design advisor) / Abe Office
Location: Tokyo

e-Front runners
富士電機
LACOSTE

Hokkaido Centennial Tower

Piercing the sky, the Hokkaido Centennial Tower was built to commemorate the development of Japan's northernmost island, which began in 1869. Previously, Hokkaido had been home to the Ainu Indigenous people whose culture and livelihood were largely wiped out by the influx of settlers from other parts of the country. Though criticized for its lack of Ainu acknowledgment, the structure's bold form became a fixture in the landscape and a meaningful landmark for many.

Located in Sapporo's Nopporo Forest Park, the project resulted from a competition won by architect Ken Iguchi of the Tokyo-headquartered firm Kume Sekkei Co., Ltd. 'We pursued a sculptural expression of strong vitality that overcomes the harsh nature of Hokkaido', said Iguchi.[29] Having deep ties to the island, the architect had firsthand knowledge of its extreme weather. Appropriately, he clad his tower with Corten steel that stood out against summer's lush greenery as well as winter's white snow.

Correlating with the memorial's timespan, the 100-metre (328-foot) high structure began with a hexagonal base – an abstraction of the ubiquitous snowflake. From there, its two halves swooped up from the ground and then, gathering momentum, soared straight upward. Stairs on either side led to the eighth level where an observation deck overlooked the city and the surrounding Ishikari Plain.

1970
2023

Architect: Ken Iguchi / Kume Sekkei Co., Ltd.
Location: Sapporo

Naha Tower Building

Completed prior to Okinawa's International Ocean Expo which opened in 1975, the Naha Tower Building became an overnight sensation. Its unusual top-heavy form immediately added flare and sophistication to downtown Naha. Not to mention much needed parking in the city's growing commercial centre where narrow streets abounded, and pavements were practically non-existent – driving here wasn't for the faint-hearted. Fronting a vast, multistorey garage (later converted to retail) in back, the nineteen-storey building faced the area's main artery, Kokusai Street, with a black cubic base balanced by a white drum on top.

More than a mere billboard, the drum contained observation decks and, best of all, a revolving restaurant. Over the course of an hour, it revealed a 360-degree view. 'You could see all of Naha', recalls the architect's son, Masaru, who ate there as a child. 'The restaurant was always full'. Aside from diners, few people entered the building since it mainly held offices, but the impact of the bold exterior extended far and wide. 'It was a symbol of Naha City,' comments Masaru.

1973
2014

Architects: Nobuyoshi Kinjo + Gendai Sekkei Co., Ltd.
Location: Okinawa

ファー
越
24h
precio
TANNING SALON
日焼け
サロン
4F
日焼
サロン
夜10時
営業中

SONY Building Osaka

Still flexing its muscles after hosting the 1964 Tokyo Olympics, Japan retooled itself as a technological powerhouse by launching Expo '70 in Osaka. Forward looking and future oriented, the exhibition site centred on a massive space frame designed by Kenzo Tange, Kisho Kurokawa's mentor, and *The Tower of the Sun*, an otherworldly sculpture of gargantuan proportions created by Taro Okamoto. It was against this backdrop that the SONY Osaka Building came into being amid the city's Shinsaibashi business district.

Looking light-years ahead of its time, Kurokawa's building – a skinny structure with a small footprint – literally towered over its neighbours alongside a multilane thoroughfare running through the city centre. Playing up these proportions, a series of exposed vertical conduits, each one different, ran up the narrow end of the building. These included glass-enclosed stairs and lifts plus shiny metal utility piping. The WCs were contained in a stack of stainless-steel boxes resembling and sized the same as the appendages made famous by Kurokawa's Nakagin Capsule Tower. Pushing these elements to the edge and placing mechanical spaces at the top yielded plenty of room for the building's core component: ten showroom floors for SONY's latest innovations.

1976
2006

Architect: Kisho Kurokawa
Location: Osaka

SONY
BROTHER
ブラザー
ミシン・編機
BROTHER
ブラザー
紀陽銀行
心齋橋筋

Origin I

In Kyoto's Nishijin district the sense of history is almost palpable. Here, timber rowhouses built centuries ago still stand shoulder to shoulder. Long and narrow, these so-called 'eel's nest' buildings combine home and workplace under one roof. Many belong to the kimono and obi sash-makers that have populated the neighbourhood for generations. Ironically, it was here that the avant garde architect, Shin Takamatsu, realized his first built work – cleverly named Origin I.

The project began when the head of an obi weaving company decided to replace their four-hundred-year-old building. Instead of the usual laundry list of room requests, the client simply asked for a work of architecture. The use of space could be decided later. 'He just said build whatever you think is best for the site', recalls the architect. Thousands of sketches later, Takamatsu proposed a three-storey granite-clad structure defined by a flat but rounded roof and a keyhole-shaped opening in front. Like kimono, which assume the shape of the wearer's body, the interior of Origin I moulded to the client's functional needs, including a triple-height entry hall at ground level and a top-floor executive suite peering out through the façade.

1981
2013

Architect: Shin Takamatsu
Location: Kyoto

Tanabe Agency Building

It is not surprising that a rock band drummer turned talent agent wanted a flashy facility to elevate the image of his company headquarters. What is surprising is that Kazuhiro Ishii supplied him with a railway bridge lookalike complete with steel supports, X-shaped bracing and rivets galore. The distinctive form of these somewhat quaint, somewhat antique, metal structures is hardly foreign to Japan. A country riddled with rivers, not to mention surrounded by seawater, Japan has excelled at all sorts of bridge construction, spanning Edo-period footbridges propped up by wood scaffolding, Meiji-era demonstrations of newly acquired civil engineering might, and more recently, dazzling steel suspension structures. But recasting the iconic bridge form as a building? That was a new one.

Hemmed in by neighbours on either side, Ishii compensated for the snug quarters with angled planes that started at street level, stepped upward and then plateaued in the middle before descending to become the building's mirror image back side. As if accentuating the site's narrowness, cross bracing ricocheted from one side of the building to the other, providing structural stamina as well as sash for the glass enclosure that turned bridge into building.

1984
2010

Architect: Kazuhiro Ishii
Location: Tokyo

3793-5600
FUSO

Kirin Plaza Osaka

Rarely do buildings have the impact of Shin Takamatsu's Kirin Plaza Osaka. This over-the-top edifice was dominated by four twenty-metre (sixty-six-foot) high light towers jutting skyward from the corners of its contrasting black granite base. Highly articulated with gridded lines and gleaming metal, the building's components fit together with mechanical exactitude and industrial precision. 'There are many ways to create something, but the one that interests me is the power hidden in machines', says the architect. In addition to epitomizing his streamlined aesthetic, this building emblemized the economic overdrive of Japan's bubble economy.

The interior was equally impactful. Commissioned by Kirin Holdings in honour of the 100th anniversary of the brewery's founding, the seven-storey building held cultural amenities as well as entertainment venues: bars, restaurants, a gallery and a theatre. It occupied a conspicuous corner amid Osaka's nightlife district where so-called eat-and-drink buildings – multistorey stacks of clubs and pubs – stand chock-a-block. Vying aggressively for customers, each one has more garish signage than its neighbours. But none rivalled Kirin Plaza Osaka. While its stone surfaces reflected the pulsating neon nearby, its pillars of light – each one generated by five thousand fluorescent tubes – glowed heroically.

1987
2009

Architect: Shin Takamatsu
Location: Osaka

an
Arbeit News
明日からQueen!
453-9111

Wakita Hitecs

Naturally, Shoei Yoh's office building for the metalware maker, Wakita Hitecs, showcased steel. Sandwiched between flat floor and roof decks, it was a rectangular swathe of column-free space that wore its structural support system on the outside. 'The motif of the building was a suspension bridge', explains professor and Yoh specialist Masaaki Iwamoto. Underscoring the nautical trope, Yoh enlisted the superior steel-crafting skills of Japan's sophisticated shipbuilding industry to produce the intricate hardware that buoyed up his building.

Hovering above street level, Yoh's glass-walled building seemed to practically float; in fact, it was held by a web of suspension cables and tension rods. These were tied to jumbo mast-shaped columns, two on each side, that anchored the building firmly to the ground. Fashioned like a gangway, lightweight scissor stairs made of metal grille ascended from the parking area below to the entrance in the middle of the building. A longtime collaborator with this client, the architect – who launched his career as an interior designer – worked with them at various scales, from offices to office goods, unsurprisingly made of metal.

1990
1993

Architect: Shoei Yoh
Location: Fukuoka Prefecture

WAKITA

Japan's Penchant for Partial Preservation

If architecture can't be saved in its original form, is it worth saving at all? There is no easy answer to this question. Keeping something is better than nothing is a frequent response in Japan – be it salvaging a select piece or rehoming an entire building. Though the impact of architectural design weakens when the ties to its original purpose or place are severed, some transplants succeed more than others. 'The value of a building is not just its façade but its inner space,' explains Kazuhiko Nishi of the Agency for Cultural Affairs. When this is addressed, even aging architecture remains relevant and acquires new vitality.

One of the most common practices is 'façadism' – the grafting of an existing building front onto new construction. This often meets with mixed reviews but can be a way to keep a building's most prominent feature. Named after the Japanese word for 'postage stamp', Kitte Marunouchi forms the base of the thirty-eight-floor JP Tower designed by Kengo Kuma. It stands opposite Tokyo Station, on the site of the 1931 Tokyo Central Post Office. Taking cues from this historic building, Kuma reinstated its white-tiled façade and wall-mounted clock at the high-rise's base, which contains a five-storey shopping mall. 'How to design the relationship of the old and new is critical', explains Kuma. Inside, the angled openings of the original concrete structural frame ring the mall's glass-ceilinged atrium – a strategy that reveals and celebrates the building's history. It feels fresh, not frozen in time. But the meaningful integration of an existing building can be hard to achieve.

Shortly after the Great Kanto Earthquake in 1923, the Japanese Government built the Dojunkai Aoyama Apartments in Omotesando. Over the years this block-long housing project morphed into a maze of tony boutiques and tiny art galleries – adaptive re-use at its grassroots best – although most of the building was sacrificed for the Omotesando Hills urban mall, which opened in 2006. The new development held onto and buffed up a segment of the original building, but it stands there like a ghost from the past.

For better or for worse, the Omotesando Hills approach enabled a slice of the apartment building to remain in situ. Nevertheless, this is the exception more than the rule. Keen to save Japan's Meiji era (1868–1912) buildings threatened with demolition, architect Yoshiro Taniguchi spearheaded the launch of Meiji Mura, an architecture-themed park where they could be resurrected. Since its 1965 opening, myriad buildings have been moved there in part or whole – the main entrance and lobby of Frank Lloyd Wright's Imperial Hotel most famous of all. Open-air museums like this do preserve buildings from the past, but what's on view is as much artefact as architecture. They are no longer living entities.

The fate of more recent buildings remains to be seen. Inevitably, parts of some will be saved. But unlike timber or even brick construction, concrete buildings are difficult to take apart and reconstitute. Until viable workarounds are conceived, their partial preservation will be debated.

(*top*) Tokyo Central Post Office, Tetsuro Yoshida, 1931.
(*bottom*) JP Tower, Kengo Kuma, 2012.

Care

08

Nurture
Support
Nourish
Tend
Minister

Namegawa Island Resort

Junzo Yoshimura was an architect game to design anything – even an entire amusement park off Chiba Prefecture's Pacific coast. A blend of tropical paradise and modern architecture, Namegawa Island was an island in name only. But it was a place apart from the routine – both figuratively and literally. 'It was absolutely different from normal Japanese life', recalls the architect's daughter, Takako Yoshimura. And that was part of its popularity and appeal. At a time when few could afford an actual island holiday, this local resort was a welcome substitute.

Nestled in and among the hilly terrain alongside the seashore, the development was approached through a tunnel. Once through the entry gate, a sequence of terraced patios and pools dotted with potted palm trees and beach parasols unfolded. It culminated in Yoshimura's wedge-shaped hotel, which surveyed the site and the ocean beyond.

A place for adults as well as kids, the resort was not only for swimming and sunbathing. It also included a zoo, an outdoor theatre for performances by hula dancers as well as the resident flamingos and, of course, plenty of built-in places for play. 'I still remember the music of the carousel', said Takako, who recalls childhood visits to Namegawa Island fondly.

1964
–UNK

Architect: Junzo Yoshimura
Location: Chiba Prefecture

Oita Medical Hall + Annex

Medical Hall
1960–1999

Annex
1972–1999

The Oita Medical Hall was the first realized work by Arata Isozaki, who went on to a remarkable career topped off by the Pritzker Prize at the ripe age of eighty-seven. But this building was finished when the architect was a mere twenty-nine years old; the ink on his Tokyo University diploma was barely dry and he didn't even have an office. Instead, he spent his days working for his mentor, Kenzo Tange, and his nights cranking out drawings for the doctors down in Oita.

Facing the city's castle moat, this heart-stopping structure featured an oval concrete tube elevated two stories above street level by chunky stilts – it reminded Isozaki of a piggybank. Looming over the shops and tile-roofed homes nearby, this was concrete used in a highly expressive, sculptural way, and a radical departure from the familiar columns and beams. While a lecture hall filled the tube, the director's office and conference rooms were tucked underneath.

Twelve years later, Isozaki was at it again – big room on top, small ones below – for the Annex that nearly doubled the facility's size. Like a gateway, the old building stood in front of the new one. This time another curved form, a tiered amphitheatre, was ringed with ribbons of clerestory windows.

Architect: Arata Isozaki
Location: Oita Prefecture

白蟻の

Izumo Grand Shrine Administration Building

Situated at the far reaches of Shimane Prefecture, the Izumo Grand Shrine compound is among the most venerated sites of Japan's Indigenous religion: Shintoism. It contains a collection of buildings whose steeply pitched roofs harmonize with the hilly terrain and timber construction coexists amiably with the forested landscape – most notably the frequently photographed Worship Hall, adorned with an immense *shimenawa* sacred straw rope. After losing one of these wooden structures to fire, architect Kiyonori Kikutake was asked to design its replacement. A proponent of Metabolism, Japan's homegrown design movement which championed the organic growth of architecture and urbanism through the subtraction and addition of its parts, Kikutake practised what he preached.

Naturally, designing for a place of such spiritual and historic importance had its challenges, especially for a modern thinker like Kikutake. Obviously, the new construction had to be fireproof, but it also had to blend with the shrine's traditional architecture. In response, Kikutake proposed a concrete building resembling the iconic form of an *inagi* rice-dying rack.

No doubt concrete was a daring choice. Even shrine officiants were surprised. But Kikutake deftly used it for bar-like components that could be factory-made and assembled on site like Lincoln Logs. In addition to evoking

1963
2016

Architect: Kiyonori Kikutake
Location: Shimane Prefecture

御守所

wood construction, this method could, in theory, enable the replacement of worn-out pieces – a strategy that dovetailed with Kikutake's Metabolist leaning as well as Izumo's legacy. Like Shintoism's important Ise Shrine, whose buildings are reconstructed every twenty years, Izumo was once the scene of ritual rebuilding.

Kikutake's kit of parts started with a pair of hefty ridge beams at the building apex and anchored at either end by boxy stair enclosures. In turn, the beams propped up slender columns that tilted inward. Creating screen-like walls, horizontal bars interspersed with strips of glass spanned between the columns. Balancing opacity and transparency, these louvred walls both shielded and admitted daylight inside.

Entered in the middle of the building, the interior was essentially a single tall space with a mezzanine. At ground level there were places for reception and offices and the double-height treasury area used to house and display sacred objects and paintings. The upper level held a ceremonial space plus preparatory rooms for the priests. Illuminated by paper pendant lights, the atmosphere was quiet and contemplative but connected to the natural world outside.

Yamagata Hawaii Dreamland

Like a mirage, Yamagata Hawaii Dreamland rose up from the rice paddies. This self-contained, futuristic concrete structure cut a sharp contrast with its idyllic setting – no doubt unchanged for hundreds of years. But what better place to test drive a newly minted architect with bold ideas? So thought a local industrialist keen for a hot spring resort with a Hawaiian theme. This concept was not entirely off the wall in 1960s Japan where economic growth was snowballing. Citizens had a little leisure time and a bit of pocket money, and many dreamed of a Hawaiian holiday. Though few could afford overseas travel, the trek up to Yamagata Prefecture was well within budget.

What greeted patrons upon arrival was an amoeba-shaped building – there wasn't a straight line in sight – with a large, open-air swimming pool in the middle. Ringing the pool were various enticements: kids' play areas, a bowling alley, restaurants, guest rooms, plus go-karts and a Ferris wheel on the roof. There was even a small zoo. Housed in an attached, glass-enclosed cone accented with palm trees, the hot spring baths were one of the biggest draws. However, because a mainly outdoor resort was a mismatch with chilly Yamagata, it vanished after just eight years.

1967
1975

Architect: Kisho Kurokawa
Location: Yamagata Prefecture

Tokumaru Children's Clinic

In Japan, where zoning laws can be quite flexible, gas stations abut cafés, parking lots touch private homes, and medical offices sometimes face shot bars. For architects, these sticky situations can be design opportunities. Such was the case when Itsuko Hasegawa combined a paediatrician's workplace and home on land adjacent to a lively entertainment district.

In lieu of the clinically cold, the doctor envisioned a warm, welcoming place where kids could be kids and their parents could relax. Hasegawa achieved this with a five-storey building containing the doctor's practice on the first three floors and his pitched roof home above. She used a hybrid structure – concrete on the bottom and steel on top – to give formal expression to this functional pairing.

Comprising the building base, the masonry separated the clinic from its surroundings by fronting the street with a solid, windowless façade. To prevent the concrete from cracking, Hasegawa created curved joint lines that visually softened the wall's hard surface and contrasted with the straight lines of the aluminium panels upstairs. Echoing this motif, arched walls gently partitioned the interior while enabling the young patients to move freely from place to place.

1978
2009

Architect: Itsuko Hasegawa
Location: Ehime Prefecture

TOKUMARU CHILDREN'S CLINIC

Taisekiji Temple Shohondo

Built at a scale and size seldom seen in Japan, let alone its religious buildings, the splendiferous Shohondo sanctuary of Taisekiji Temple was a marvel to behold. It had grandeur. It had monumentality. And it was completely mind-blowing. Especially its gargantuan suspended roof, whose swooping form was thought to resemble a crane taking flight. This was the crown jewel of the Nichiren Buddhist complex situated near the foot of Mount Fuji.

Like a European cathedral, the sanctuary was preceded by a sequence of symmetrical formal spaces culminating in its high altar. First came the outdoor forecourt centred on a pool with the profile of a lotus blossom and a fountain in the middle. From there worshippers progressed through an open colonnade featuring five colossal columns, each one topped with an umbrella-shaped cover.

Upon entering the Shohondo, ramps ascended into the single-storey sanctuary. Fanning out from the dais were an astonishing 5,400 seats for congregants; another 600 for the priests surrounded the altar. Overhead, the roof dipped down in the middle but from there soared up and outward along its central axis. Supported by massive, splayed trusses ringing its base, this awe-inspiring ceiling was a spiritual expression and structural wonder all in one.

1972
1998

Architect: Kimio Yokoyama
Location: Shizuoka Prefecture

Sweat

09

Compete

Train

Pump iron

Work out

Kick

Throw

Run

National Stadium

Readying Tokyo for the 1964 Olympics brought many urban as well as architectural upgrades. Overhead expressways were constructed, the Shinkansen bullet train made its debut, and numerous buildings arose, including this open-air arena for track and field. With great fanfare, it was here that the Olympic opening and closing ceremonies were held – events that celebrated international athletes, and signified Japan's re-entry to the global arena after recovering from the devastation of World War II.

Some of the Olympic venues, including this arena, were in Jingumae, a central Tokyo district where athletics facilities have existed since the Taisho era (1912–1926). Golf swings were perfected, baseball was watched and various events were enjoyed in this stadium – that is, until the run-up to the 2020 Tokyo Olympics when the decision to replace it was finalized.

Unsurprisingly, this conclusion was not uniformly well-received. While some welcomed the construction of a state-of-the-art stadium, others protested vigorously – a first for Japan. Ultimately, the building was taken down, though not before the original, now aging, Olympic athletes were invited back for a last lap.

1958
2015

Architect: Mitsuo Katayama
Location: Tokyo

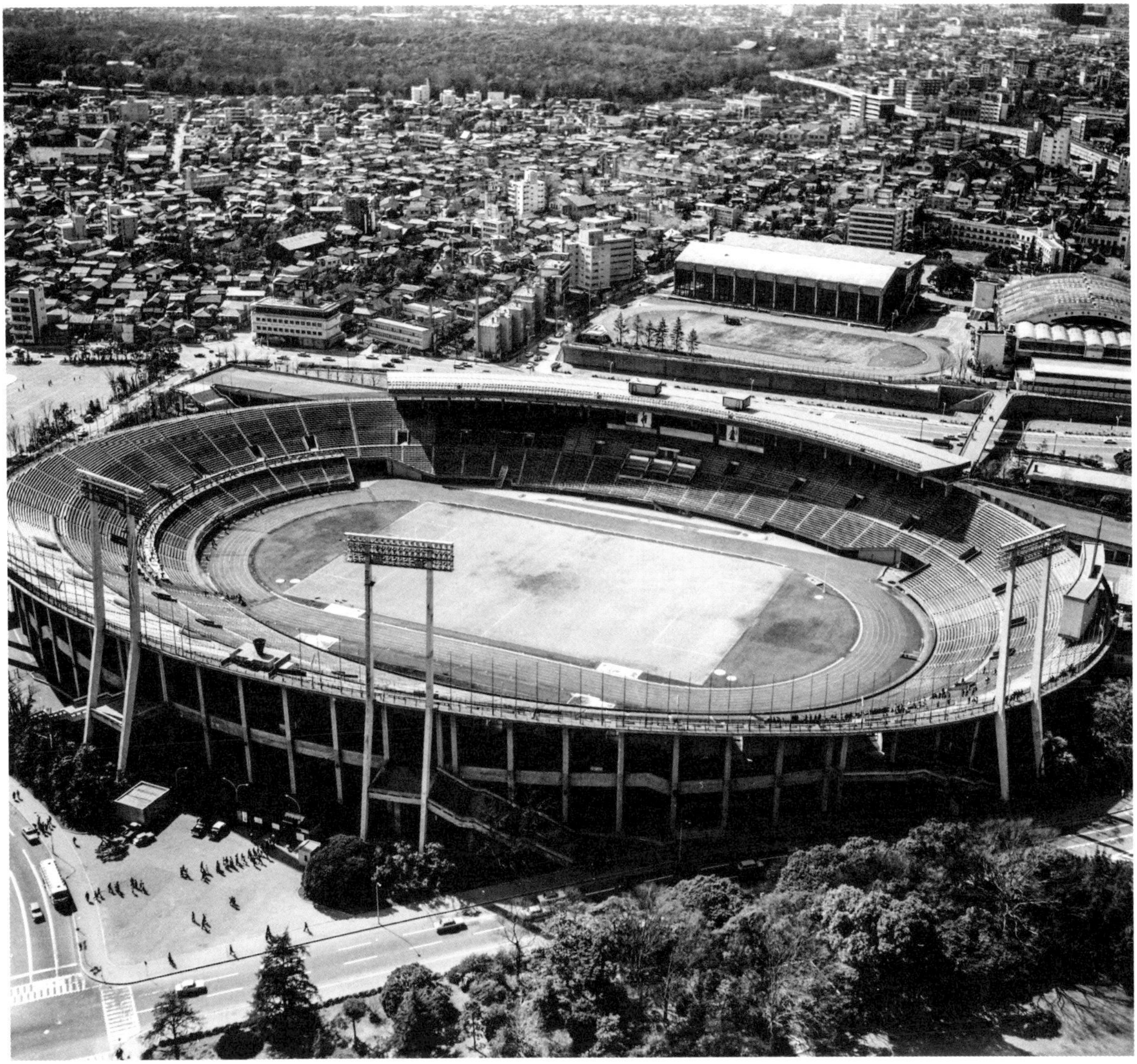

Enoshima Yacht Harbor Clubhouse

It was the Olympics that gave rise to this building, and it was the Olympics that brought it down. Designed by Yoshiro Taniguchi with Mizuki Yamada, a competitive sailor-turned-architect, the building was constructed for the 1964 Games' yacht races. But by the time planning for the 2020 Games launched, the wind had gone out of its sails and a replacement was deemed necessary.

Situated on a small island facing Sagami Bay, Taniguchi's pentagonal building consisted of three wedge-shaped blocks, each one roofed with a pair of folded sail-shaped planes. As even keeled as a ship's hull, the boxy lower level held storage, lockers and other services for the boaters. The double-height upper floor featured the entrance hall, restaurant, bar and a generous terrace whose swimming pools invited relaxation. For those hankering after salt air, an elevated walkway led to an observation tower where the sea extended as far as the eye could see.

1961
2014

Architects: Yoshiro Taniguchi / Mizuki Yamada
Location: Kanagawa Prefecture

Totsuka Country Club Clubhouse

With its spectacular swooping roof, this clubhouse was unbeatable, earning top scores for both elegance and brawn. But where climate control was concerned, it wasn't up to par. The up-turned eaves and full-height glass walls did little to block the sun, and after eighteen holes, club members wanted to quench their thirst sheltered from the strong rays. Kenzo Tange was not known as a golfer but his mentor, Hideto Kishida, was an avid linksman – who designed both golf clubhouses and courses – and a Le Corbusier enthusiast. It was Kishida who landed Tange this commission, according to architectural historian Saikaku Toyokawa, and it was Kishida who introduced the Swiss architect's concrete buildings to his students.

Here, concrete formed the clubhouse's roof plus the six, enormous, exterior columns holding it up. Separating structural skeleton and skin – a traditional idea born anew – a glass box enclosed the interior. The main member areas included a restaurant and lounge with changing rooms underneath. These segued into a separate but connected concrete box with an inwardly folded roof. It contained a traditional bath as no golf outing in Japan is complete without a post-game soak.

1961 –UNK

Architect: Kenzo Tange
Location: Kanagawa Prefecture

Shimonoseki Municipal Gymnasium

With sparkling, scale-like shingles and a gaping façade, this building resembled a gigantic fish breaking the water's surface. But the uniqueness of the gym was more than skin deep. 'It was probably the only one in the world designed solely by a structural engineer', speculates engineer Masao Saitoh, who carried out the project under Yoshikatsu Tsuboi.

Typically, architects design buildings and engineers make them stand up. But in Japan the two disciplines are often closely fused – a mode of practice embraced by Tsuboi from the start of his career. Though he was not an architect, Tsuboi helped shape buildings right from the beginning, especially those needing large, column-free spaces. He is best known for collaborating with Kenzo Tange on several of the architect's early works, including the Hiroshima Children's Library, Ehime Prefectural Hall, and Yoyogi National Stadium built for the 1964 Tokyo Olympics. Looking at the arena's dynamic roof, it is hard to know where the architecture ends and the engineering begins.

Japan in the early 1960s was a busy time for building design. Fuelled by the country's robust economy, construction was going at a fast clip. It was a great time to be an architect. This was the scene when Shimonoseki's gym came to be. To host athletics competitions, concerts and other events, the city wanted a building the likes of which had never been

1963
2024

Architect: Yoshikatsu Tsuboi
Location: Yamaguchi Prefecture

seen. But the budget was low and the schedule super tight. Putting one person in charge of both architectural and structural design was an efficient solution. And, given his track record, Tsuboi had the necessary know-how to do both.

Naturally, the backbone of the building was its unique structural skeleton whose pointed arches at the front morphed into rectangular frames in back. These supported the three triangular planes forming the gym's exterior: one tilted roof and two curving sides covered with squares of gold-coloured aluminium.

Following the roof configuration, the building opened with a four-storey façade and tapered down to a single-storey block in back where ping pong was played. The main arena was in the middle with the bulk of its built-in bleachers stepping up towards the building front. 'Climbing those stands was like climbing a mountain', recalls architect Keita Takimoto, who grew up in Shimonoseki. But no one complained. 'People loved the design but also the functionality', says Saitoh.

Kagawa Prefectural Gymnasium

Dry docked on massive pylons, this hulking concrete edifice looks more like Noah's Ark than a municipal gym. The world, let alone Takamatsu City, had never seen anything like it. And nor will they ever again if the building is dismantled – a possibility that looms large.

In fact, this Kyushu Island city has not one but two Kenzo Tange works. A riff on conventional column-and-beam construction, the Kagawa Prefectural Government Office has been preserved, expanded and is very much in use. By contrast, the gym's enigmatic form was closed years ago after it was deemed structurally unfit. One fatal weakness is its heavy, saddle-shaped roof that curves in two directions. This configuration may be the reason the ceiling is too low for competitive volleyball and badminton. For a city planning to host professional sports and other crowd-pleasing events this simply wouldn't do.

Retrofitting was considered by local authorities but rejected. Plus, bulky structural shoring might mean the building could no longer serve as a gym. Though the construction hoarding may go up and the building come down, diehards in favour of preservation and repurposing have yet to concede. In the words of the American baseball player, Yogi Berra, 'It ain't over 'til it's over'.

1964
—TBD

Architect: Kenzo Tange
Location: Kagawa Prefecture

Shizuoka Prefectural Kusanagi Gymnasium

What do Stevie Wonder, Diana Ross and Whitney Houston all have in common? Among other things, each one played the Kusanagi Gymnasium – a gathering spot for athletes, spectators and music aficionados. Accompanied by outdoor stadiums and baseball diamonds, this arena was part of a sports park punctuated by paths and ponds. During the period of its construction, communities had the resources for athletics facilities, citizens had the time for leisure activities, sports education was increasing, and gymnasiums were being built countrywide. Every town wanted one.

In Shizuoka, this took the striking form of an octagon with concrete piers at each corner to support the zig-zag-shaped roof. Composed of eight steel-plate segments creased like origami, it culminated in a central skylight. Inside, the oblong playing area was hugged on two sides by ascending rows of seating. There was nary a view-blocking column anywhere – a triumph of a long-span structural system. But this may have been the building's Achilles heel too. After being deemed structurally unfit, the gym was levelled and its site returned to parkland.

1966
2016

Architects: Yamashita Architects & Engineers
Location: Shizuoka Prefecture

Notocho Hot Spring Spa

Perched at the tip of the Noto Peninsula on the so-called 'backside' of Japan, the secluded town of Mawaki is a place steeped in history – and a place where locals habitually steeped in hot water. Populated by farmers and fishermen, the area is also home to an important archaeological site dating from the Jomon period (14,000–300 BCE) when pit dwellings – literally holes in the ground capped with pitched roofs – were the norm. More hut than house, these wall-less buildings protected inhabitants from the harsh winters and accommodated comfortably to the undulating terrain. In keeping with this landscape and its history, Reiko Tomita created a public bathhouse composed of roofs – some curvy, some pointy, all distinctive.

'We wanted to express each element differently', explains Tomita. Affectionately called 'Tyrannosaurus' and 'Stegosaurus' respectively by the architect, the men's bath was topped with a soaring tower while the women's featured an ovoid dome that practically hugged the ground. Inside, both baths were supported by hefty wooden beams and columns that contributed to the steamy, shadowy atmosphere. Additional roofs articulated the two changing rooms, tatami-floored rest area and the lobby – a freeform space that united all the disparate pieces.

1993
2013

Architects: Reiko Tomita / Atelier Zo / Team Zoo
Location: Ishikawa Prefecture

Kannabe Hot Spring Spa

Be it in a deep tub at home, a communal bath in the city or a hot spring spa in the country, soaking in hot water is a favourite pastime in Japan. More than a place to simply wash, the bath is a place for relaxation. For that purpose, the Toyooka town government created this public facility for the local farming community. Spilling over from one to the next, it was a network of indoor and outdoor pools of various types and sizes. During the summer heat as well as the winter snows, the refreshing waters drew crowds.

Facing the street, the spa started with several small house-sized buildings containing changing rooms. From there a footbridge crossed the long outdoor pool, with the tallest bath, the Forest of Columns – an enclosed wooden structure topped by a steeply angled roof – at one end. 'We wanted to create a forest-like place', explains Reiko Tomita, Atelier Zo principal. Within the pool, the architects planted a grid of chunky, tree-like columns clothed in square tiles. 'People would hide behind them and then suddenly appear', recalls Tomita. 'It was lots of fun.'

1994
2013

Architects: Reiko Tomita / Atelier Zo / Team Zoo
Location: Hyogo Prefecture

Repurposing – Not Everything that Goes Up Comes Down

Japan has already lost many architectural treasures, but not everything that goes up comes down – some buildings do get renovated and updated. Others get refurbished and then repurposed entirely, resulting in some unexpected, and often delightful, pairings of old and new.

Compared to Europe or the United States, refurbishment happens, but with less frequency. In Japan, repairs can be expensive, especially when invasive seismic reinforcing is required. And when worn-out buildings fall short functionally, taking them down might appear to be the best option. Though some types have more staying power than others, even multi-storey department stores are vulnerable to demolition. But the destruction of buildings carries steep economic as well as environmental costs. Not to mention the risk of public outcry – occasionally protesting the removal of a beloved building makes a difference. In 2016, when Junzo Sakakura's Museum of Modern Art, Kamakura – Japan's first public modern art museum – was under threat, its fate looked bleak. But after citizens spoke out, this masterpiece of 1951 was restored, retrofitted for earthquake safety and renamed. The reborn Kamakura Bunkakan Tsurugaoka Museum reopened in 2019.

Requiring less architectural intervention, the easiest transitions occur when new functions simply take up residence in old buildings, hermit-crab-style. Combining nostalgia and novelty, these solutions often yield enticing places to work, shop, eat and stay. Consider the classroom converted into a Kyoto coffee shop, the bathhouse that became a popular Tokyo art gallery or an Onomichi warehouse recycled as a hotel for bikers and their wheels.

Regarding form as well as function, some buildings are more amenable and more available to being repurposed. Commercial and hospitality industries adapt well to existing space. Shops have built-in longevity since they are comparatively easy to update and undergo frequent renovations. Due to Japan's dropping birth rate, schools countrywide have been consolidated or

(*top*) Onomichi U2/ Hotel Cycle, Suppose Design Office, 2014.
(*bottom*) Kamakura Bunkakan Tsurugaoka Museum (née Museum of Modern Art, Junzo Sakakura, 1951).

closed outright, leaving behind a plethora of buildings with good bone structure. And warehouses containing vast partition-free space are like blank canvases that can accommodate all kinds of new uses.

In each case there is currency attached to the building's former life. Keeping some hardware fittings, finishes, and even furnishings, is part of the charm. This also resonates with *mottainai*, a repurposing practice from the past that remains embedded in Japan's collective psyche. At a time when resources were limited, inventive ways to utilize food scraps, threadbare cloth and other daily use goods developed. The connection to the past can be a boon for contemporary businesses catering to consumers. These days, anything with a Showa era (1926–1989) vibe has cachet.

Given their appeal, both renovation and repurposing could be growth areas for Japan. More creativity and more willingness to experiment will aid the cause. 'The know-how is not enough in Japan', explains Professor Yuki Ozawa. 'But bit by bit, the thinking is changing.' Hopefully in time to recycle more of the country's architectural treasures.

スバル

Move

10

Travel
Ride
Drive
Sail
Climb
Go

Idemitsu Apollo Gas Stations

For many architects, small buildings are opportunities to experiment – especially when greenlit by the client. Between 1956 and 1962, the president of the Idemitsu Kosan Co., Ltd. petroleum company commissioned Junzo Sakakura to create fifty-three gas stations – all unique. At that time, Japan's automotive industry was moving into high gear and its citizens were acquiring cars at record speed. Appropriately, Sakakura's attention-grabbing fresh takes were fuelled with the excitement of car travel.

Built countrywide, the stations shared several common features. Functionally, all were engineered for ease of movement between the street and the pumps. And visually all incorporated the brand's red and white colour scheme, plus its dashing logo featuring the stylized profile of the Greek god Apollo, authored by graphic designer Hiroshi Ouchi in 1950. Perhaps the sun god was a particularly apt image in the land of the rising sun.

For the roofs, however, Sakakura went into overdrive – each one being equally dramatic. While triangulated panels topped the Hiroshima outpost, umbrella-shaped circular covers hovered over the Ikebukuro station. Fun and futuristic, they reflected Japan's forward momentum.

1956
–UNK

Architect: Junzo Sakakura
Locations: Tokyo and other locations

(*top*) Ikebukuro station.
(*overleaf*) Namba station.

APOLLO

Mount Senkoji Observation Tower

For those in search of retro Japan, the seaside town of Onomichi is the place to go. Its covered Showa-era *shotengai* shopping street has become the proverbial *shuttergai* – a mash-up of Japanese and English referring to stores that are closed (shuttered) for good. Its residential hillside remains riddled with narrow pedestrian paths but *akiya* (abandoned houses) abound. And for sixty-odd years, Takeo Satow's charming umbrella-shaped Mount Senkoji Observation Tower overlooked it all.

Accessed by ropeway, the three-storey lookout sat at the summit of Mount Senokoji where it commanded panoramic views of the rolling hills nearby, the picturesque Seto Inland Sea in the distance and everything in between. The tiny tower consisted of two parts: a cylindrical core enclosing a spiral stair, above which sat a circular glass-enclosed restaurant with a roof deck on top. The round room was supported from below by spokes extending out from the concrete core, umbrella-style. No stranger to public works, Satow may be better known for large city halls and expansive civic centres but, despite its diminutive size, this little landmark was dear to locals and tourists alike.

1957
2021

Architect: Takeo Satow
Location: Hiroshima Prefecture

Idemitsu Takamatsu Gas Station and Office

As commissions go, the gas station may not carry the cachet of a civic centre or a concert hall. But with Togo Murano behind the wheel, the lowly petrol stand became a vehicle for design creativity. Over the course of his career, Murano racked up many miles with the oil and gas giant, Idemitsu Kosan Co., Ltd. In addition to some twenty gas stations around the country, he authored administrative offices and even the private guesthouse of the company founder and his childhood friend, Sazo Idemitsu.

As in other locations, Murano integrated the Takamatsu gas station with company offices. The building's most distinctive – and decorative – feature was its dynamic wavy roof, clad with traditional Japanese copper shingles with a green patina. This segmented, circular cover hovered protectively over the two-storey drum-shaped building below. On either side, the circular form linked to single-storey boxes. Open to the street and identified with the iconic Apollo logo sign, one held the consumer service station. Though unusually fancy for an oil outpost, the petal-shaped roof was a favourite and frequent Murano motif.

1962
–UNK

Architect: Togo Murano
Location: Kagawa Prefecture

Meishin Expressway Toll Gate

The origins of Japan's national expressway system stemmed from the five major roads set up by the Shogunate during the Edo period (1603–1868). These became the backbone of the highways created in 1919, which led to the expressway network built after World War II. According to the Ministry of Land, Infrastructure, Transport and Tourism, Japan had 130,000 car owners at that time but by 1957 there were a whopping two million. The economy was going strong, people could afford cars and domestic automobile production had begun. Clearly, better highways were needed. Their construction was spearheaded by the Japan Highway Public Corporation with an all-star design advisory team, including architects Kenzo Tange, Kunio Maekawa and Junzo Sakakura.

Connecting Nagoya and Osaka, the first segment to open was the Meishin Expressway whose toll gate was designed by Sakakura and became the prototype for expressways throughout Japan. His clean design consisted of six independent red booths interspersed with three slender pillars to support the roof. With its cantilevered ends and light blue underside, the roof practically floated. Marking the journey's starting point, this light, elegant form matched the freedom of the open road.

1964 –UNK

Architect: Junzo Sakakura
Location: Aichi Prefecture

9
8

Shinjuku West Plaza + Shinjuku Station West Building

Shinjuku
West Plaza
1966–2022

Shinjuku
Station West
Building
1967–2024

Shinjuku is among the busiest commercial districts in one of the most crowded cities on earth. At its epicentre stands Shinjuku Station where a mind-boggling number of subways, trains and buses converge daily – the result of transit line extensions and urban development after World War II. This turned the station into a major transportation hub with people going every which way all day and well into the night. Designed to mitigate the area's growing pains, Junzo Sakakura's Shinjuku West Plaza and Shinjuku Station West Building deftly unified the physical fabric and orchestrated movement patterns that separated pedestrian and vehicular traffic but kept everyone moving in the right direction.

Equally adept at designing furniture as city infrastructure, Sakakura worked comfortably at every scale. As his prolific career coincided with Japan's period of stratospheric economic growth, he completed several projects amalgamating buildings, city planning and transportation nodes, including Tokyo's Shibuya Station, Osaka's Namba Station and Nara's Kintetsu Station. But his contribution to Shinjuku was by far the most prominent and, undoubtedly, the most heavily trafficked.

The development's first stage was the West Plaza, an expansive concourse abutting Shinjuku Station. Its defining visual feature was a pair of open vehicular ramps, one up and

Architect: Junzo Sakakura
Location: Tokyo

あさり市
ARTMENT STORE

ODAKYU
SALE
ODAKYU CLEARANCE
小田急クリアランス
POLICE

one down, which spiralled between the underground and street levels. While parking and pedestrian walkways were below, rows of bus terminals were aligned neatly above. Both connected to the broad, pavement-lined avenues on either side. Between the ramps, burbling fountains helped enliven the underground space. 'Even from the basement we could see the sky', recalls the architect's daughter, Miho Kida. Elsewhere, hollow concrete conduits directed daylight and fresh air downward while perking up the Shinjuku streetscape with their sculptural forms.

Loosely containing the plaza, tall buildings sprung up along its perimeter, including the Keio and Odakyu department stores. Promoted by private railroad companies, both filled the empty real estate above their respective trainlines. Occupying much of Sakakura's Shinjuku Station West Building, his Odakyu store formed the plaza's elegant backdrop and an angled street wall with its gridded façade. Internally, stairs and lifts linked shoppers to the basement level train lines which, in turn, connected to the plaza's underground pathways.

(*p. 281*) Shinjuku West Plaza.
(*left*) Shinjuku Station West Building and Shinjuku West Plaza from below.

Osaka Kuzuha Pedestrian Bridge

One of the greatest industrial designers of all time, Sori Yanagi may be best known for his moulded plywood Butterfly Stool. But throughout his prolific career, Yanagi worked on everything from cookware and cutlery to fire hydrants and footbridges. 'He wasn't just making things for everyday life', explains Koichi Fujita of the Yanagi Design Office. 'He was making things that were out in the world'. As much sculptural artefacts as urban gestures, Yanagi's various bridges garnered their own exhibit at Tokyo's tony Matsuya Design Gallery in 1968. Most of these brilliant designs remained unbuilt. But Kuzuha, a 'bed town' commuter suburb midway between Kyoto and Osaka, set that straight.

With the grace of a traditional wooden bridge, Yanagi's blue steel structure crossed the town's two-way, tree-lined thoroughfare, separating cars from people without blocking the distant mountain view. Angled inward at either end, the symmetrical arch rose gently, reaching its apex in the centre. Shallow stairs integrated with monolithic form enabled pedestrians to cross comfortably from one side to the other. Created when Japan's economy was going gangbusters and urban development was rampant, this bridge was a small concession to beauty.

1972 –UNK

Architect: Sori Yanagi
Location: Osaka

Tokyo Auto

Typical of Team Zoo, a collective of independent architectural ateliers named after different animals, Tokyo Auto, a used car dealership, took its inspiration from the local flora and fauna. Its wavy roof was supported by branch-like steel underpinnings and bird-shaped column capitals. The exuberance of this edifice was enough to stop traffic.

Located near a highway interchange, the two-storey building held a street-level showroom, a balcony-level café and multipurpose public spaces. Essentially, it was a car dealership-cum-civic-centre. This tidy arrangement enabled motorists to cruise the merchandise below while *kaffeeklatsches* and community meetings happened above.

With its laser-cut plywood furniture and shiny silver ceiling, the interior was no less impressive. But Tokyo Auto's most visible selling point was its roof, which Atelier Mobile principal, Kinya Maruyama, terms 'the identity of architecture'. Though the undulating form was inspired by the area's hothouses for growing *kampyo* gourds, the gleaming aluminium surface was straight-up automotive. While its deep overhangs provided shade, eyebrow-shaped windows shed light on the showroom below.

1984
2023

Architects: Kinya Maruyama / Atelier Mobile / Team Zoo
Location: Tochigi Prefecture

Harumi Passenger Ship Terminal

The point of departure and entry for ocean-bound travellers, the Harumi Passenger Ship Terminal was a landmark loved by many. But one didn't need to board a boat to enjoy this building. It was certainly a beacon of interest for visitors to the shores of Tokyo Bay but also for the steady stream of cars crossing Rainbow Bridge nearby. Sadly, the bridge's opening just two years after the terminal's construction sounded the port building's death knell. The increasing size of cruise ships coupled with the height limit for boats passing beneath the bridge rendered the terminal all but obsolete.

The terminal's demolition occurred just thirty-one years after its completion, which commemorated the fiftieth anniversary of the opening of the Tokyo Port to international trade. The building was surrounded by a grand plaza whose dizzying black and white chequerboard patterns were built-in super graphics – a Takeyama favourite. While immigration proceedings occupied the terminal's base, an outdoor promenade stepped up to the top-level observation deck looking out to sea. Covered with a pyramid of white lattice, the terminal became a house of light at night.

1991
2022

Architect: Minoru Takeyama
Location: Tokyo

MK Higashi Gojo Gas Station

A historic post town turned contemporary 'bed town', Yamashina has long been an important transportation node on the route connecting Kyoto and Edo (as Tokyo was called in the pre-modern era). Appropriately, it was here that Shin Takamatsu's MK Higashi Gojo Gas Station once stood.

Parallel to the road, roof-covered rows of gas pumps led up to the oblong station, which shimmered like a silver roadster with red trim. Its two entrances, one for cars and one for people, led to the service and the retail areas respectively. Linking these two halves was a shared office with internal doors opening to either side. Flanking the store entrance, symmetrical stairways ascended to a crescent-shaped gallery on the second floor. Visible from afar, this over-the-top geometry echoed the circular entry vestibule at street level. The whole shebang was rendered in glass and red steel – the company's signature colour. There was no need for an explicit logomark or flashing neon. 'The gas station itself was a sign', explains Takamatsu, who often came here to refuel his green Volvo.

1987
–UNK

Architect: Shin Takamatsu
Location: Kyoto

Power/on.
Power/on
MK石油

Power/on.
wer/on.
バッティングセン
テニス・バッティング・卓球・ゲーム・

Afterword

This book presents just a small sampling of Japan's buildings from the post-war period and beyond that no longer exist. Nationwide, many have been lost and many more are threatened with extinction. At this time, even prominent landmarks, such as Tokyo's National Theatre of Japan designed by Hiroyuki Iwamoto of the Takenaka Corporation, are in limbo. It is hard to predict the future of buildings like these. Even more so for those with less public presence – not all can, or even should, be saved. The root causes of their demise are unlikely to change – earthquake safety is always going to be a major concern, wear-and-tear is a reality – and money, well, it talks. What can change is the value assigned to Japan's recent buildings and the acknowledgment of the impact of their demolition on Japan's architectural legacy.

It is not that Japan does not treasure its architectural history. Far from it. As early as the 19th century, venerated temples and shrines made of wood began garnering public funding and support. Scrolling ahead to the 1960s, Japan's robust economy triggered a construction boom which contributed to the demolition of Western-style buildings from the Meiji era (1868–1912). But the destruction of some ultimately stimulated the protection of others. Subsequently, the historic preservation initiatives of Japan's Agency for Cultural Affairs broadened. Outdoor architectural

National Theatre, Hiroyuki Iwamoto/Takenaka Corporation, 1966.

Mitsubishi Ichigokan,
Mitsubishi Estate Co., Ltd.,
2009.

museums were readied for rehoming aged structures of various sorts. And the Mitsubishi Ichigokan, a Queen-Anne-style office building from 1894, was completely levelled in 1968 – only to be rebuilt from scratch in 2009. One may not cotton on to any of these approaches, but each demonstrated an increased appreciation of Japan's architectural heritage.

For the time being, Japan's hard-surfaced, sharp-cornered concrete buildings have yet to win the affection granted to the storybook appearance of red brick or the intricate joinery of handmade wood construction. While this situation can lead to the destruction of such concrete structures, it may also enable their altering and repurposing – another means of revitalizing vintage buildings, at least in part. But full-on preservation remains elusive when architecture is undervalued or even unvalued. '[W]hen does [a building's] cultural importance trump practical considerations?' probed architecture critic Nicolai Ouroussoff.[30]

Encapsulating time and place, buildings are receptacles of history, memory and taste. Their loss not only changes the physical landscape but deprives future generations of experiencing these important works of architecture for themselves. Perhaps Japan's demonstrated cycle of destruction of historic buildings followed by their renewed appreciation and preservation is in the process of repeating itself. Perhaps the loss of Japan's modern buildings to date will stimulate the preservation and survival of those that remain.

Notes

1. Hiroyuki Suzuki, 'The Historical Background of Postwar Public Architecture in Japan' in John Zukowsky (ed.), *Japan 2000: Architecture and Design for the Japanese Public* (Prestel, Munich, New York, 1998), p. 21.

2. Naomi Pollock, 'Newsmaker: A Conversation with 2024 Pritzker Prize Laureate Riken Yamamoto' in *Architectural Record*, 5 April 2024.

3. Jonathan M. Reynolds, *Maekawa Kunio and the Emergence of Japanese Modernist Architecture* (University of California Press, Berkeley and Los Angeles, 2001), p.163.

4. Arata, Isozaki, *GA Architect 06, Arata Isozaki 1959-1978* (A.D.A Edita, Tokyo, 1991), p. 66.

5. Peter Landers, 'RIP: Japanese Bank Tower that Embodied Nation's Industrial Might' in *Wall Street Journal*, 26 September, 2016.

6. Hiroshi Hara, *Kenchikubunka*, June 1968, p. 99.

7. Fumihiko Maki, 'Four Schools' in *Space Design* (Kajima Institute Publishing Co., Ltd., Tokyo, June 1979), p. 78.

8. Fumihiko Maki, 'Marine Life Park for Expo 1975' in *Space Design* (Kajima Institute Publishing Co., Ltd., Tokyo, June 1979), p. 54.

9. Seng Kuan and Yukio Lippit, *Kenzo Tange: Architecture for the World* (Lars Müller Publishers, Zurich, 2012), p. 108.

10. Kenzo Tange, 'In Answer to the Questions about the Metropolitan Government Office' in *Tange by Tange* (TOTO Publishing, Tokyo, 2015), p. 78.

11. Saikaku Toyokawa, 'Kenzo Tange as Seen through the Eyes of Kenzo Tange' in *Tange by Tange* (TOTO Publishing, Tokyo, 2015), p. 23.

12. Ibid., p. 78.

13. Noboru Kawazoe, *Contemporary Japanese Architecture* (Kokusai Bunka Shinkokai, Tokyo, 1968), p. 59.

14. Ibid., p. 78.

15. Seng Kuan, 'A Genealogy of Structural Design in Japan' in *Structured Lineages: Learning from Japanese Design* (The Museum of Modern Art, New York, 2019), p. 22.

16. Ibid., p. 23.

17. Jonathan Reynolds, *Maekawa Kunio and the Emergence of Japanese Modernist Architecture* (University of California Press, Berkeley and Los Angeles, 2001), p. 202.

18. Takashi Hasegawa, 'The Still-pounding Waves of Sea of Japan' in *The Architecture of Youji Watanabe* (Shinkenchiku-sha Co., Ltd., Tokyo, 1985), p. 13.

19. Kenzo Tange, *SD Review* (date unknown).

20. Itsuko Hasegawa, *ITSUKO HASEGAWA Section 2* (Itsuko Hasegawa Architecture Atelier Co., Ltd., Tokyo, 2015), p. 224.

21. Ken Tadashi Oshima, 'Elevating Environments' in *The Wright Imperial Hotel at 100: Frank Lloyd Wright in the World* (Kajima Publishing Co., Tokyo, 2023), p. 171.

22. Kiyoshi Seike, *The Details of Kiyoshi Seike: Doors and Windows*, ed. Design System, (Shokokusha, Tokyo, 1984).

23. Hiroshi Watanabe, *The Architecture of Tokyo* (Edition Axel Menges, Stuttgart/London, 2001), p. 151.

24. Hiroshi Matsukuma (supervisor), Kazuto Kasahara et al. (eds.), *The Prolific World of Togo Murano: Architectural Models* (Seigensha Art Publishing, Inc., Kyoto, 2016), p. 121.

25. Kenneth Frampton and Kunio Kudo (eds.), *Nikken Sekkei: Building Modern Japan 1900-1990* (Princeton Architectural Press, New York, 1991), p. 111.

26. Ibid.

27. Naomi Pollock, *Japanese Design Since 1945* (Harry N. Abrams, Inc., New York, 2020), p. 248.

28. Yoshinobu Ashihara, *The Japan Architect* (Shinkenchiku-sha Co., Ltd., Tokyo, August 1966), p. 78.

29. Ken Iguchi, *Hokkaido Centennial Memorial Tower* (Shinkenchiku-sha Co., Ltd., Tokyo, June 1971), p. 203.

30. Nicolai Ouroussoff, 'Future Vision Banished to the Past' in *New York Times*, 6 July, 2009.

Index

Page numbers in *italics* refer to illustrations

Picture Credits

a = above; b = below
Sources of illustrations by PAGE NUMBER

1, 45, 47, 136, 149, 151, 215, 217, 237 © Tomio Ohashi; 2-3, 221 © Nacása & Partners; 4-5, 127, 140, 251 Photo Chuji Hirayama © Jiro Hirayama; 6-7, 109 Shigeo Ogawa; 8, 61, 62-3, 175 Courtesy Design System archive; 12 © Michiko Uchida; 14, 281 Keystone Press/Alamy Stock Photo; 15 Courtesy Former Kagawa Prefectural Gymnasium Rebirth Committee; 16 Ned Snowman/Shutterstock; 17 yannick luthy/Alamy Stock Photo; 22-3 ITSUKO HASEGAWA atelier; 24-5, 235, 241, 242-3 © Javier Vives; 26, 35, 36, 37 Courtesy Arata Isozaki & Associates; 29 Yoshio Watanabe; 31, 33a, 199, 277 Photo Wafu-Kenchiku-Sha. Collection KIT Museum and Archives; 33b, 39, 79, 114, 135, 145, 155, 161, 191, 209, 213, 219 Courtesy Ura-kun; 41, 42-3 Yoshio Shiratori/ZOOM; 48 pisaphotography/Shutterstock; 50, 75, 76-7, 131 Kaneaki Monma; 53, 54-5, 87, 89, 90, 91 Kenzo Tange Archives © Michiko Uchida; 57, 58-9, 67, 125, 263, 264-5 Eiji Kitada; 65, 132-3, 187 Shokokusha Publishing Co., Ltd.; 69, 70-1, 81, 173, 249 Shinkenchiku-sha; 73, 289 Kinya Maruyama; 83 © Toshiharu Kitajima; 84, 93 Keiti Kimura; 95 Courtesy Shimizu Corporation; 97 Courtesy Hiroshi Matukuma; 99, 231 © Osamu Murai. Courtesy Kumi Murai (Osamu Murai Photo Archives); 101, 103 Courtesy Tatsuo Iso; 105 Gendai Sekkei; 107, 261 Courtesy Shuji Yamada; 111 Motoi Niki, Nacása & Partners Inc.; 113a Courtesy Great Kanto Earthquake.com; 113b Kokubo Works/Alamy Stock Photo; 117, 119 Courtesy Tokyu Corporation; 118 Photo courtesy Noribumi Kitamura © F.L.C./ADAGP, Paris and DACS, London 2026; 121 Wafu-Kenchiku-Sha. Collection KIT Museum and Archives; 123 Fumio Murasawa; 129 Osugi/Shutterstock; 139, 141 Courtesy Urban Renaissance Agency; 143, 259 © Akio Kawasumi; 146-7 Arai Masao; 153 Takeshi Sato(Youji Watanabe Office); 157 Newscom/Alamy Stock Photo; 159 Mitsumasa Fujitsuka; 163 Thomas Bland/Alamy Stock Photo; 165 © Yusuhara Town; 167, 168 Courtesy Imperial Hotel, Ltd.; 170, 193, 194-5, 205 MIWA Kokyu; 177, 233, 234, 296 Thomas Kyhn Rovsing Hjørnet/Alamy Stock Photo; 179 REUTERS/Kimimasa Mayama/Bridgeman Images; 180 SZ Photo/Kristina Eriksson/Bridgeman Images; 183 Masayuki Yamashita/Alamy Stock Photo; 184 Nina Alizada/Shutterstock; 185 Photo Yukio Yoshimura. Courtesy Maekawa Architects; 189, 206, 207 © Kochi Prefecture, Ishimoto Yasuhiro Photo Center; 196, 203a SHOTENKENCHIKU-SHA Publishing Co., Ltd.; 201, 202, 203b Kawasumi,Kobayashi Kenji Photograph Office; 211 Askanioff/Alamy Stock Photo; 223 N studio. Courtesy Shoei Yoh Archive; 225a Courtesy Postal Museum; 225b Trevor Mogg/Alamy Stock Photo; 226, 239 ITSUKO HASEGAWA atelier; 229 Kindai Kenchiku; 244, 253, 254, 255 Courtesy TAISEI Corporation; 247 Three Lions/Getty Images; 257 John Barr/RIBA Collections; 267a Picturesque Japan/Shutterstock; 267b Toshiyuki Yano; 268 ZUMA Press, Inc./Alamy Stock Photo; 271 Collection of the National Archives of Modern Architecture, Japan; 272-3, 279 Courtesy Sakakura Architects & Engineers; 275 Courtesy Jun Aoki; 282 World Discovery/Alamy Stock Photo; 285, 286-7 © Yanagi Design Office; 291 Courtesy Mamo; 293, 294-5 © Katsuaki Furudate; 297 Jui-Chi Chan/Alamy Stock Photo

About the Author

NAOMI POLLOCK is an American architect and author who writes about architecture and design in Japan. Her articles have appeared in publications on both sides of the Pacific such as *A+U*, *Dwell*, *Jutakutokushu*, *Kinfolk*, *Wallpaper** and *Architectural Record*, for whom she is a Contributing Editor. She has also written numerous books, including *Jutaku: Japanese Houses*, *Sou Fujimoto*, *Japanese Design Since 1945: A Complete Sourcebook* and *The Japanese House Since 1945*. In addition, she was the editor of *NUNO: Visionary Japanese Textiles*. In recognition of her contributions as a journalist and critic, she was invited into the College of Fellows of the American Institute of Architects in 2018.

Acknowledgments

This book would not have been possible without the kind assistance of many people. For starters, I would like to thank my colleagues at Thames & Hudson: Lucas Dietrich, Augusta Pownall, Helen Fanthorpe, Tatiana Wilde, Julie Bosser and Matt Watson-Young. Each of you enabled me to turn my initial concept into this completed book. I owe a special thank you to Anabel Navarro for sourcing the photos so expertly and to the book's designer, Daniele Roa, for blending the visual and the written so elegantly.

I am extremely grateful to the many architects, engineers, academics, government officials, critics and photographers who helped me along the way. I am particularly thankful to Jun Aoki, Michino Aoyama, Wahei Aoyama, Taro Ashihara, Collection of National Archives of Modern Architecture, Japan, DOCOMOMO Japan, Former Kagawa Prefectural Gymnasium Rebirth Committee, Hiroyasu Fujioka, Kouichi Fujita, Mitsumasa Fujitsuka, Itsuko Hasegawa, Isao Hashimoto, Yoshiki Hirao, Jiro Hirayama, Nobuko Inaba, Tatsuo Iso, Masaaki Iwamoto, Kota Kawasaki, Miho Kida, Masaru Kinjo, Eiji Kitada, Atsushi Kitagawara, Noribumi Kitamura, Shuko Koike, Yoshiki Kondo, Kengo Kuma, Yasuhiro Mandai, Kinya Maruyama, Hiroshi Matsukuma, Kumi Murai, Kazuhiko Nishi, Yuki Ozawa, Yuko Saito, Masao Saitoh, Takeshi Sato, Kazuyo Sejima, *Shinkenchiku*, Rie Someya, David Stewart, Taisei Corporation, Mayumi Takahashi, Shin Takamatsu, Keita Takimoto, Tsuyoshi Tane, Yuko Saito, Ano Sato, Sanae Tobita, Tokyu Corporation, Reiko Tomita, Saikaku Toyokawa, Michiko Uchida, Toru Ueda, Susumu Uraminami, Michel van Ackere, Javier Vives, Koji Yagi, Hinata Yamaguchi, Riken Yamamoto, Namiko Yamauchi, Koichi Yasuda, Takako Yoshimura, Koichi Yumizaki.

Lastly, I would like to thank Eve, Abby, Alex, Beth and, most of all, David to whom this book is dedicated. I could not have completed this publication without your sage advice, sense of humour and constant support.

On the cover:
(*front*) Hotel Sofitel Tokyo, Kiyonori Kikutake, 1994-2008 by Neil Setchfield/Alamy Stock Photo
(*back*) Nakagin Capsule Tower, Kisho Kurokawa, 1970-2022 © Tomio Ohashi

p. 1: SONY Building Osaka, Kisho Kurokawa, 1976
pp. 2-3: Kirin Plaza Osaka, Shin Takamatsu, 1987
pp. 4-5: Gakushuin University Auditorium, Kunio Maekawa, 1960
pp. 6-7: Higashinihonbashi Police Box, Atsushi Kitagawara, 1992
p. 8: Nomura Display Co., Ltd., Kiyoshi Seike, 1965
pp. 22-23: Bizan Hall, Itsuko Hasegawa, 1984
pp. 24-25: Taisekiji Temple Shohondo, Kimio Yokoyama, 1972
p. 26: Fukuoka Sogo Bank Oita Branch, Arata Isozaki, 1967
p. 50: National Aquarium, Okinawa, Fumihiko Maki, 1975
p. 84: Asahikawa City Hall, Takeo Satow, 1958
p. 114: Ginza Theatre Building, Kiyonori Kikutake, 1987
p. 136: Nakagin Capsule Tower, Kisho Kurokawa, 1970
p. 170: Dai-ichi Kangyo Bank Head Office, Yoshinobu Ashihara, 1981
p. 196: San-ai Dream Centre, Shoji Hayashi/Nikken Sekkei, 1962
p. 226: Tokumaru Children's Clinic, Istuko Hasegawa, 1978
p. 244: Shimonoseki Municipal Gymnasium, Yoshikatsu Tsuboi, 1963
p. 268: Shinjuku West Plaza, Junzo Sakakura, 1966

First published in the United Kingdom in 2026 by Thames & Hudson Ltd, 6-24 Britannia Street, London WC1X 9JD

First published in the United States of America in 2026 by Thames & Hudson Inc., 500 Fifth Avenue, New York, New York 10110

For full picture credits, see page 302

Cover and interior layout designed by Daniele Roa

EU Authorized Representative: Interart S.A.R.L.
19 rue Charles Auray, 93500 Pantin, Paris, France
productsafety@thameshudson.co.uk
interart.fr

A CIP catalogue record for this book is available from the British Library

Library of Congress Control Number 2026931609

ISBN 978-0-500-02828-5

01

Printed in China by RR Donnelley

MIX
Paper | Supporting responsible forestry
FSC® C144853